Jane Cave

Poems on Various Subjects

Entertaining, Elegiac, And Religious

Jane Cave

Poems on Various Subjects
Entertaining, Elegiac, And Religious

ISBN/EAN: 9783744713634

Printed in Europe, USA, Canada, Australia, Japan

Cover: Foto ©Lupo / pixelio.de

More available books at **www.hansebooks.com**

Mifs JANE CAVE.

POEMS

ON

VARIOUS SUBJECTS,

ENTERTAINING, ELEGIAC,

AND

RELIGIOUS.

By JANE CAVE.

WINCHESTER:
Printed for the AUTHOR, by J. SADLER.
M,DCC,LXXXIII.

To the SUBSCRIBERS.

YE gen'rous patrons of a female's muſe,
    Ere you my works with ſtudious eye
    peruſe,
My pen would firſt in humble ſtrains impart
The genuine dictates of a grateful heart:
Thanks to my friends—and ſhould my labours
       pleaſe,
Crown'd are my wiſhes, and my heart's at eaſe;
My time improv'd, my muſing hours well ſpent,
If theſe conſpire to give my friends content:
But * Seward, Steele, or Moore, hope not to
      ſee,
With gentle candour read the Author's Plea.‡

* Celebrated Poeteſſes.——‡ The firſt Poem.

THE
NAMES
OF THE
SUBSCRIBERS.

OXFORD.

A

REV. Mr. Alleyne
Rev. Mr. Agutter
Mr. Adams
Annefley
Amphlett
Alexander
Abbott
Aldridge
Apperley
Mrs. Atterbury
Adee
Auftine
Mifs Adams

B

Rev. Dr. Bathurft, Canon of
Chrift Church, 2 Cop.
Rev. Dr. Borrough
Rev. Mr. Bathurft, 3 Cop.
Burton
Barnard
Buckland
Bradly
Barker
Barrington
Barnes

Rev. Mr. Booth
Bond
Beake
Bright
Hon. Mr. Bingham
Mr. Cha. Burton
Burgefs
Bell
Batt
Buller
Budge
Buckerfield
Baillie
Barton
Brooke
Beaver
Blackmore
Jaines Brown
Bracher
Bofanquet
Burn
Buttlar
Bull
Brockman
Bennett
Batley
Wm. Benfon
J. Bacon

1

Mr.

Mr. Blundell
Blackftone, Queen's Coll.
Blackftone, New Coll.
N. Barton
Barrett
Mrs. Brodrick
Borrows
Mifs Burton

C

Rev. Dr. Chapman, Prefident of Trinity Coll.
Rev. Dr. Cook
Rev. Mr. Cooke
Crowe
Coke
Clap
Collinfon
Hon. Mr. Cathcart
Tho. Caldecott, Efq.
Mr. Crawfood
Coleman
Richard Cox
Chamberlayne
J. Copfon
Clavering
W. Carr
Coates
Chorley
Cornifh
Curtis
Cooke
Carey
Cowley
Calland
Caker
Cartwright
Commeline
Clarke
Compton
Challen

Mr. Courand
Clayton
Cobannel
Mrs. Caftle
Couper

D

The Lady of the Rev. Dr. Dennis, Vice Chancellor of Oxford
The Lady of the Rev. Dr. Dennifon, Principal of Mag. Hall
Rev. Dr. Dixon, Principal of Edmond Hall
Rev. Mr. Davis, Bal. Col.
Davis, Mert. Coll.
Douglas
Mr. Drummad
Daintry
Dale
Donne
Deedes
Dardigareve
Dakin
T. Davis
Dallaway
Dornford
Davis
Davie
Devalangin
Davis, jun.
Mrs. Downes

E

Rev. Mr. Everleigh, Provoft of Oriel Coll.
Rev. Mr. Edwards
Mr. Edmonftone
Edwards, Ch. Ch.
Etton
Elliott
Edwards, Hert. Coll.
Mr.

Mr. Ebdell
    Edwards, Pem. Coll.
    Edwards, Jesus Coll.
    Eyton
    Eccles
    Ebdon
Mrs. Etty

F

Mr. Fletcher, Mayor
Rev. Dr. Fothergill, Provost
    of Queen's College, 2
    Copies
Rev. Mr. Fothergill
    James Fothergill
    Filks
    Finch
    Ford
Mr. Frankland
    Filmer
    Fhurlow
    Filmer, C. C. C.
    Fortescue
    J. Fisher
    Fernghough
    Flamank
Mrs. Fothergill
    Ford

G

Rev. Mr. Gould
    Griffith
    Godfrey
    Goutch
Mr. Gabell
    Gascoyne
    Grosvenor
    Gordon
    Greenhill
    Guard
    Gaitham
    Gray
    Gresley

Mr. Geary
    Gurdon
    Goode
    Gregory, Exeter Coll.
    Gore
    Griffith
    Glover
    Grubbe
    Gregory
Miss George
    Grant

H

Rev. Mr. Holland
    Hughes
    Heeghway
    Halse
    Hayes
Mr. Harper, G. C.
    Harris
    Hyde
    Harrison
    N. Hill
    Hall
    Holner
    Hungerford
    Holyoake
    Tho. Honiatt
    Hopkins
    Hill
    Hurdis
    Hutton
    Howell
    Hooker
    Haskett
    Hulme
    Hurst
    Holt
    Hill
    Hawkins
    Hughes
    Hume, 2 Copies

Mr.

Mr. Headley
Hunt, Trin. Coll.
Harbin
Hunt, Pem. Coll.
Hereford
Hildyard
Hatton
J. Hutchinſon
Mrs. Hornſby
Hawkins

J

Rev. Mr. Ingram
Joham
Jones
Johnes
Mr. Ilbent
Jones
Jeſton
Ireland
Jones, jun.
Mrs. Jenner

K

Rev. Mr. Keeple
Knight
Kirrick
Knight, P. Coll.
Kilner
Kening

L

Hon. Mr. Legg
Hon. Mr. Littleton
Rev. Dr. Long
Rev. Mr. Lichfield, M. Coll.
Lichfield, W. Coll.
Lawthian
Landon
Lediard
Mr. Lee
Lindſay
Lockwood
Rob. Leigh

Mr. Le Meſſerier
Lyſons
J. Langley
Leighton
Mrs. Lowny
Ludbey
Miſs Lawrance

M

Rev. Dr. Mortimer, Rector
of Lincoln Coll.
Rev. Mr. Montagu
Moulding
Maſſon
Matthews
Maſſingberd
Mr. Martin
Meckham
Moſs
Milner
Meakin
Milward
Muckleſton
Martin
Matthew
Mathew
Millward
Mead
Methold
Muſgrove
Meredith
Marſhall
Mrs. Morrell
Mayo

N

Hon. Frederick North
Rev. Dr. Nowell, Principal
of St. Mary's Hall
Rev. Mr. Newman
Thó. Newman
Nicholl
Mr. Newman

Mr.

Mr. E. Nares
 Newman
 Nash
 Nettleship
 G. Nicholas
 Newton
  O
Rev. Dr. Oglander, Warden of New College, 3 Copies
Mr. Oliver
 Oldsworth
 Ogle
  P
Rev. Mr. Parr, Fel. of C. C.
 Prosser
 Pole
Mr. Peck
 Prince
 Pearson
 Piddocke
 Pulventoft
 Payne
 Parker
 Percivall
 Papillon
 Plater
 Paget
 Phillips
 Pasons
 Phelps
 Pitt
 Pemberton
 Powell
 Parsons
 Peachy
 Patterson
 Palmer
 C. Plunknett
 Paul
Mrs. T. Prickett

Miss Peck
  R
The Rev. Dr. Randolph, Principal of Albion-Hall
The Lady of the Rev. Dr. Randolph, President of C. C.
Rev. Dr. Reading
Rev. Mr. Roberson
 Routh
 Radcliffe
 Ruyeter
 Rolls
Mrs. Rowney
 Redwood
Mr. Rawley
 Raddish
 Roberson
 Rouquet
 Rupell
 Ramnecy
 Raisbeck
  S
Rev. Mr. Smallwell, Canon of Christ Church, 2 Copies
Rev. Dr. Sheffield, Provost of Worcester Coll.
Rev. Mr. Sissmore
 Stratford
 Shaw
 Smith
 Spencer
 Shore
 Scott
Edwin Sandys, Esq.
Mr. Scott
 Shutt
 Smith
 Stafford

Mr.

Mr. Smyth
Samuel
Spearing
Shawe
Stone
Sharp
Shaw
Smith
Shore
Saltren
Stevers
Slaney
Stuart
Mrs. Suger
E. Seely
Mifs Smith
Ann Smith
Sydenham

T

The Hon. and Rev. Dr. Tracy, Warden of All Souls, 3 Copies
Rev. Mr. Tanner
Tefh
Turner
Totham
Tahourden
Twopenny
Mr. Tomkins
Trollope
Tomkip
W. E. Taunton
Thomfon
Tyrwhitt
Trebeck
E. Tawney
Tomkins
Toke
Traleton
Trollepe
Tree

Turner
Trevelyan
Mrs. G. Treacher
Tucker, Q. Coll.
Tucker, Bal. Coll.
Mifs Taylor
Tuck

V

Rev. Dr. Vivian
Mr. Vigor
Ventnis
Vaffall
Vernon
Vaughan
Upton

W

Hon. Mr. Windfor
The Lady of the Rev. Dr. Wetherell, Mafter of Univer. Coll.
Dr. Wall
Rev. Mr. White
Wood
Warton
Watkins
Wifdome
Williams, W. C.
Williams, J. C.
Watfon
Welles
Woodroffe
Mr. Willes
Wingfield
W. Willes
Warren
White
Wrey
Wenman
Wroughton
Williams, M. Coll.
Wood

Mr.

Mr. Watter
Webbe
Wood
Worlcombe
Weftern
Woodhann
Wood, Queen's Coll.
Y
Rev. Mr. Yeatman
Mr. Yates

WINCHESTER.

A

MR. Anderfon
Mr. Applegarth
Mr. J. Auftin
Mifs Anderfon
B
Rev. Mr. Ballard
Bathurft
R. Botten, Efq.
Enfign Barlow
Mr. R. Barlow
Barker
Beckett
Brereton
Bowles
Burdon
Borman
Mrs. P. Bathurft
Barlow
Berkenhout
Beckett
H. Blackftone
Burgat
Bayfpoole
Bifhop
Mifs Barlow
M. Barlow
L. Barlow
C. Barlow

Mifs Blannerhafs
Bingham
C
His Grace the Duke of
Chandos, 7 Copies
Her Grace the Duchefs of
Chandos, 7 Copies
Lady Charnock
Mr. T. Cooke
Cave
Carter
Curtes
Mrs. Clarke
Chiverton
Mifs Collings
D
John Dofwell, Efq. Mayor
Hon. Mrs. Dormer
Mr. John Dowling
Dunn
Mrs. Dodfworth, 3 Copies
Durnford
Dofwell
Mifs Draper
E
Mr. Earle
Eaft
G
Lord Gray
Rev. Mr. Gauntlett, 2 Cop.
Gabell
Goddard
C. Gauntlett, Efq.
P. Gauntlett, Efq.
Mrs. Gamon
Mifs Ginkins
H
Rev. Mr. Huntingford
Howley
Mr. Howley
Hutchinfon

Mrs.

Mr. Harfield

Hilman

Hooper

Mrs. Hair

Hide

J

Mr. Joules

K

F. C. Kirby, Efq. S. at Law

Mr. Kentifh

C. Kirby

W. Knapp

Mrs. Ker, 3 Copies

Knott

Kimber

L

Lady Caroline Leigh

Rev. Mr. Lowth, P. of W.

Dr. Littlehales

Mr. Lyford

H. Lloyd

Mrs. Lee

Leathes

Lovegrove

A. Line

Mifs Lee

M

Rev. Mr. Mence

Dr. Mackitrick

Thomas Middleton, Efq.

Mr. Milner

Mrs. Methara

Morrifon

Mofs

Meader

Moody

Mifs Mears

N

The Right Hon. Earl of
Northington, 7 Copies

Rev. Mr. Newbolt

Rev. Mr. Norman

Mr. Newbolt

O

Admiral Sir Chaloner Ogle

P

Rev. Mr. Price

Mr. Parry

W. A. Phelp

Mrs. Price

Pawle

Mifs Pyott

H. Pyott

Parkhurft

R

Lady Rivers

Sir Richard Reynell

Rev. Mr. Richmond

John Richurft, Efq.

Mrs. Richards

Rogers

Raven

S

James Serle, Efq.

Mr. R. Serle

T. Serle

Serle

Mrs. Sturges

Sparfhott

Scoby

Sadler

Mifs Sterck

T

Hon. Mr. Thynne

Rev. Mr. Tawney

Mr. Thomas

W. Thomas

V

Mr. Vokes

W

Rev. Dr. Warton, M. of
W. Coll.

Rev.

Rev. Mr. Williams
        Webb
Mr. Weftlake
        W. Walldin
        Wetherell
        Wool
Mrs. Warton
Mifs Warton
        Wools
        Wheatly

Y

Rev. Mr. Yaldon
James Yaldon, Efq.

SOUTHAMPTON.

A

WM. Andrews, Efq.
        Mifs Alderfey
Mifs A. Alderfey

B

Mr. Brice
        W. Brackftone
        Bernard, Surgeon
        L.-Ballard
        W. Barnard
        T. Barnard
Mrs. Bridges
        Budd
Mifs Brice
        Binmore

C

Mr. Cropp
Mrs. Champion
        Cropp

D

Rev. Mr. O. Davies
P. De Carteret, Efq.
Mr. W. Drake
Mrs. Daman
        Day

E

Mr T. Evans
Mrs. Everitt
        J. E.

F

Dr. Frazer
Valentine Fitzhugh, Efq.

G

Mr. Grierfon
        Greenftreet
Mrs. Greenftreet

H

Lady Hughes
Rev. Mr. Halton
Mr. J. Hall
Mrs. Hague
        Howard
        Hoedly
        Hamond
        Hull
        Hookey

K

Rev. Mr. Kingfbury
Mrs. Kynafton

L

Wm. Ludlow, Efq.
Major Le Marchant
Mr. T. Lys
Mrs. Le Hunt

M

Rev. Mr. Mant
Mr. Moncton
        C. Mills
        J. Mobbs
Mrs. Mills
        Meffer
        Martin, fen.
Mifs Morris

N

Mr. Noble, Mayor
Mifs Norris

P

Mrs. Pitt
Perkins
Mifs Purbeck

R

Mr. Rice
Mrs. Reed
Raymond

S

Rev. Mr. Scott
Capt. Samfon
Mr. Stappers
Sadleir
Mrs. Shorley
Simpkins
Mifs St. John

T

Mr. W. Taylor
Mrs. Thomas, 2 Copies
Tarrant
Taylor
Mifs Taylor
C. Taylor

V

Mrs. Valabra

W

Rev. Mr. Woodford
E. B. Wollftoncraft, Efq.
Mr. J. Ward
Waring, Surgeon
Wylds
Mrs. Watfon
Woodyear
Mifs Watts
Wallis

NEWPORT,

A

REV. Mr. Atkins
Mr. W. Angle

Mifs E. Abbott

B

Philip Ballard, Efq,
Mr. R. Brown
Bayly
Wm. Baker
R. Barlow
Wm. Bouzell
R. Baffett, Surgeon
Wm. Bouyell
Mrs. Ballard
E. Browfe
Mifs E. Bowden

C

Mr. Wm. Clarke
Richard Cooke
Tho. Cooke
Rt. Clarke, Attorney
R. Clarke, ditto
! Cowlam, Surgeon
Wm. Cooke
Mrs. Crooke
Mifs Clarke
Clab

D

Rev. Wm. Dickenfon
Mr. Rich. Drake
Wm. Drake
P. Dodd
Day
Mrs. E. Duglas
S. Davidfon
Duckett
Daw

E

Mrs. Elliott

G

Capt. Grace
Mr. Greves
J. Gumm
Mrs. M. Goodive
Gregory

H

Lady Holmes
Mr. Hull
Mrs. E. Hayward
    Mary Hall
    Haddon
    Harman
Miss Heaton

J

Mr. Jerom
    J. Jolliffe
    Wm. Jones
Mrs. Jolliffe

K

Mr. J. Kirkpatrick

L

Mrs. Lalow

M

Mr. Robert Miller.
    J. Mallett
Mrs. Major

N

Mr. P. Nichols
    Richard Newbery
Mrs. Noles

P

Capt. Pyott
Mr. Thomas Pittis
    E. Partridge
    W. Pedder
    Porter
    J. Perry
Mrs. Pinhorn
    Popham
    Frances Pike

R

Mrs. E. Roberts
    J. Roberts
    Rogers
    Roch

S

Mr. Wm. Sheath

Mr. J. Smith
Mrs. Sheath
    E. Simms
Miss M. Shipman

T

Mr. Trattle, Mayor
    J. Tiller
    Wm. Tucker
Mrs. E. Trattle
Miss M. Bridges

U

Mr. J. Upward

W

Rev. Mr. Worsley
Mr. John Welman
    J. Wray
Mrs. M. Wavell
    Wavell
    Whitehead

C O W E S.

A

Mr. Andrews
    Mr. Ash
Mrs. Alley

B

Mr. Blackford
Mrs. Blandford
Miss Banister
    Butterworth
    Baskerville

C

Mr. Cushen
    J. Cooke
    Civil
    Chiverton
    Wm. Cushen
Miss Corke

D

Mr. James Deacon
    Deacon

Mrs.

Mrs. De la Francis
Miss Daniells

F
Mr. Fabian -
Mrs. Francis
Miss Fabian

G
Mrs. Gely

H
Mr. Daniel Hill
    Wm. Holloway
    Harris
Mrs. Harrington
    Haddon
    Hewitt

J
Mr. Jackson
    H. Javes
Mrs. Jacob

K
Mrs. Kent

M
Mr. Mallett
Mrs. Mackenzie
    M'Culloch
    Maund

P
Mrs. Parkman

R
Mr. Roe
    Rossey
    C. Rotsey

S
Mr. Shepherd
    Spreets
    Speden
Mrs. Sime
    Simms
    Stephens

T
Mr. Thomson

W
Mr. J. Wellstead
    Leonard Wincey
Mrs. Wincey

PORTSMOUTH.

A
Mr. Aylward
    Mr. Adams
Mr. Avery
    Adams
Mrs. Alford
    Alford
    Allcock
    Asmond
    Allian
    Allian
    Adams
    Ansell
    Arnold

B
Mr. Burnett
    Barker
    E. Binstead
    Brackstone
    Baker
    Binsteed
    Baldy
    Boyes
Mrs. Broughton
    Bosee
    Brown
    Backhouse
    Burrell
    Brain
    Bowley
    Ballard
    Best
    Burlace

Mrs

Mrs. Brine
    Bruges
    Bolton
    Buſkell
    Barefoot
    Bagnoll
    S. Brown
    Barton
    Buſbridge
    Burnett
    Bacon
    Biſſett
    Byerley
    Brain
    Broughton
Miſs Bedford
    Batchelor
    Budden
    H. Boiſrond

C

Sir John Carter
Rev. Mr. Cooley
Capt. Chalmers
Mr. Cowcher, Druggiſt
    Wm. Cox
    Compton
    Cox
    Carter
    Wm. Carter
    Cooley
    Cooke
    Carter
    Curtis
    Cuzens
    Collins
    Couſens
    Charmon
    Cox
Mr. Cockton
    Coker
Mrs. Curier

Mrs. Chudleigh
    Cunningham
    Churcher
    Charters
    Cave
    Criſp
    Cowdery
    Champion
    Crow
    Cooper
    Coſins
Miſs Crookſhanks
    Cocks
    R. Cocks
    Cobden
    Cuallett

D

Mr. Deacon
    Dewey
    Danford
    Davis
Mrs. Dawle
    Dundaſs
    Denton
Miſs Dawſon

E

Mr. Elliott
    Edwards
    Elgar
Miſs Elliott
    Eyer

F

Mr. Freeman
    Freeland
    Floyd
    Foond
    Fincham
    Ford
    Fuller
Mrs. Frankling

Miſs

Miss Fenn
     Fry
        G
Mr. John Godwin, Mayor
     Greenway
     Gransmore, 2 Copies
     H. Grant
     Gauntlet
Mrs. Gray
     Grigg
     Gibbens
     Garrett
     Grossmith
     Gill
     Gregory
     Green
     Gillam
     Glandening
     Grafham
Miss Grant
        H
Lady Hood
Lady Hamilton
George Huish, Esq.
Lieut. Holmes
Mr. Horsey
     Hay
     Hancock
     Holt
     Higgens, jun.
     Hickley
     Hobbs
     Hoar
     Haylor
     Hayne
     Hill
     Halsted
Mrs. Hector
     Hillyar
     Hurry
     Hulke

Mrs. Harward
     Hunt
     Hewett
     Hunter
     Hammond
     Hill
     Hawker
     Hendry
     Heslop
     Holdstock
     Hillyer
     Hollis
     Hammond
     Hart
Miss A. Hunt
     Hinton
     Herring
     Hornby
        J
Mr. Johnson, Surgeon
     Jubber
     Jeffery
        K
Mr. Kennett
     J. Kingett
Mrs. King
     Kember
        L
Mr. Thomas Lyed
     Lawson
     Lear
     Legg
Mrs. Lyons
     Lawrence
     Ladd
     Loup
     Legg
     Leeke
     Long
     Lovell
     Luke

                           M

M

Rev. Mr. Morce
Mr. Muirhead
 Meredith
 Miall
 Millard, Surgeon
 Mitchell, ditto
 Marshalls
 Morey
 Martin
 Morley
 Morgan
 Moran
 Money
 Mills
 Mitchell
 Meffer
 Monday
Mrs. Moriaty
 Mountain
 Mouatt
 Merritt
 Morfe
 Macbean
 Mayby
 Mofes

N

Hon. Mrs. Napier, 3 Copies
George Nunns, Efq.

O

Rev. Mr. Orange
Mrs. Ofborn

P

Admiral Sir Thomas Pye,
 3 Copies
Mr. Player
 Pike
 Peers, Attorney at Law
 Polhill
 Primate
 James Paffard

Mr. Priftock
 Palmer
 Perrin
Mrs. Palby, 2 Copies
 Pearce
 Purkis
 Peace
 Porter
 Pitt
 Pope
 Pepper
 Pafley
 Poole
 Porter
Mifs Poore

R

Mr. Reed
 Ramfey
 Rule
 Rule
Mrs. Rowe
 Read
 Rookfby
 Reading
 Robfon
 Read
 Roe
 Robertfon
Mifs Ramfay

S

Mr. Sabeue
 Scurth
 Smith
 Spencer
 Smith
 Sanders
 Stephen
 Stone
 Spurrell
Mrs. Smith
 Sharp

Mrs.

Mrs. Snook
Sibley
Smith
Skeat
Shugar
Smith
Stanton
Shepherd
A. Smith
Sandys
Simpſon
Steill
Stephen
Miſs Shaw
Shepherd
T
Mr. E. Turner
Tolfree
Taylor
Tribe
Tattum
Teed
Trend
Mrs. Temple
Taylor
Thomſon
Temple
Tracy
Miſs Treleven
Teeſdale
U
Mr. Upton
Vidol
Veck
Mrs. Vaſs
Miſs Varlo
W
Mr. Weſton
Wheeler
White
G. White

Mr. Woolfe
White
Williams
Willſon
Watkins
Wade
White
Wallis
Mrs. Wiſdom
Williams
White
Wiggins
Webb
Woodman
Whitly
Winſon
Whitiar
Whitfield
Whetaker
Y
Mrs. Yatman

GOSPORT
A
MR. Adams
Mrs. Arminer
Mrs. Aſhford
Allan
Adgman
B
Mr. Biddlecomb
Blamire, 2 Copies
Badge
Boys
Billett
Burnett
Beaty
Bonar
Mrs. Bird
Barton
Bradly

Mrs.

Mrs. Badge
    Boulton
    Ball
    Buckland
    Bowden
Miſs Bedford
    Bligh
    Buckland
    Bingham,
    Blundells

C

Vincent Corbet, Eſq.
Mr. Collins
Mrs. Caſtleman
    Collins
    Creaſe
Miſs Curry
    Carter

D

Lady Douglas
Mr. Danford
    Dods
    Drane
Mrs. Dalton
    Duncan
    Daman

E

Admiral Evans, 3 Copies
James Evans
Mrs. Elliſon
    Elliott
Miſs Eldridge

F

Mr. Robert Faulkner
Mrs. Figg
    Finſby

G

Mr. Griſt
    Gilbert
    Grey
Mrs. Graham

Mrs. Goodriff
    Griſt

H

Mr. Huiſh
    Harper
Mrs. Hill
    Hayter
    Handely
    Hendley
    Hall
    Hanly
Miſs Howford
    Hollis

J

Mr. Jellicoe
    Jewell
Mrs. Jordan
    Johnſton
    Jurd

K

Mr. Kneller

L

Mr, Ledgard
    Ledſtone
Mrs. Lewis
Miſs Lowley
    Lee

M

Mald. March
Mr. Midford
    Morſe
    Marchall
    Maſon
Mrs. Marſhall
    Maſon
    Moubrey
    Merritt
    Matthews
    Maſon
Miſs Mountford
    M'Kindey

N
Mr. Neilſon
 Norriſh
Mrs. Norris
O
Mr. Orchard
P
Mr. Wm. Page
 Parker
Mrs. Pedder
 Parſons
Miſs Peachy
 Piercy
R
Mr. Redman
Mrs. Roberts
 Rook
 Reeves
Miſs Roper
 Randall
S
Mr. Smith
 Smith, jun.
Mrs. Stanfield
 Salt
 Sutton
 Shoveer
 Salter
 Silveſter
 Simpſon
Miſs Searley
 Shivers
T
Mr. Timmings
Mrs. Tither
U
Dr. Vaughan
Mrs. Vaughan
 Veaſey
 Vaines
 Underwood

Mrs. Utterſon
W
Mr. Wilkinſon
 J. Wigley
 John Whitear
 Whitcomb
 Weſtbrook
 Weſt
 Waller
Mrs. Waddy
 Woodman
 Waldron, 2 Copies
 Wareham
Y
Mrs. Young

FAREHAM.

A
Mr. Albeck
 Mrs. Altarrow
B
Lady Benett
Mr. Barney
 Blutherwick
Mrs. Bargus
D
Lady Dent
Mrs. Duglas
F
Mr. Franklin
Mrs. Franklien
 R. Fall
G
Mr. Goodive
Mrs. Gayton
 Godein
H
Mr. Henderſon
Mrs. Hodge
 Hobſon

Miſs

Miſs C. Hawker

J

Mrs. Johnſon

K

Mr. Knight
John Knight
Miſs Kneller

M

Rev. Mr. Mercer
Mr. Maſon
Mrs. Montagu

N

Mr. Newman

P

Mr. Parſons
Perry
Mrs. Parſons
Porter
Phillips
Miſs Parker

R

Mr. Ralfs

S

Mr. Sparkes
Mrs. Stares

T

Mr. Threſher
Miſs Taylor

W

Rev. Mr. Wools
Mr. Wigleſworth
Mrs. Wallis

WICKHAM.

MR. Engliſh
Mr. Prior.
Capt. Weir
Mrs. Atkins
Bradburn
Callaway

Mrs. Garnier
Maidman
Tyrwhitt
Woodrow
Miſs Jacobs

WALTHAM.

REV. Mr. Bale
Mr. Bullock
Mr. Churcher
Cook
Cole
Donniger
Rev. Mr. Duſautoy
Mr. Fox
Jennings
Jonas
Capt. Lee
Mr. J. Penford
Richards
Villians
Rev. Mr. Walters
Mrs. Barfoot
Hart
Ann Jones
Woodman

ALRESFORD.

MR. Aſlett
Mr. Bonall
Mr. Bradly
Bugby
Harley
John Hinden, jun.
Knapp
Rev. Mr. Maſters
Lady Parker
Prangnall
Shawford
Soper

Mr.

Mr. Wright
Wynn
Mrs. Aflett
Buller
Dancaster
Edwards
Green
Harnefs
Mifs Fifher
Holden
Maria Holden
Nevill
Terry

NEWBURY.

SIR Jofeph Andrews
Rev. Mr. Beft
—— Cooft, Efq.
T. Cowflad, Efq.
Mr. Hawkins
Capt. Howdell
Rev. Mr. Merchant
Parry
Ofman Vincent, Efq.
Lady Andrews
Lady Craven, 3 Copies
Mrs. Davies
Grigs
King
Merriman
Penrofe
Reidford
Sainfbury
Mifs Hine
May

ABINGDON.

MR. Bedwell
Mr. Blake

Rev. Mr. Cleoburey
Mr. Curtis
Jofeph Fletcher
Thomas Fletcher
Kent
Rev. Mr. Lake
Mr. Lewis
Moore
Rev. Mr. Stevenfon
Mrs. Nafh
Rofe
Tomkins
J. Tomkins
W. Tomkins
Tombs
Mifs Harding
Kendall
Stephens

WHITCHURCH.

MR. Barker
Rev. Mr. Blair
Rev. Mr. Garnett
Jofeph Portal, Efq.
Mrs. Meadows
Streatwell
Thorngate
Mifs Hayter
Philips

WOODSTOCK.

MR. Bennet
Mr. Coles, Mayor
Rev. Mr. Hind
King
Kidding
Mrs. Brooks
Ingram
Scriven

Mrs.

Mrs. Walker, 2 Copies
    Woodhull
Miss B. Ingram
    M. Ingram

SALISBURY.

A

REV. Mr. Adams
   Mr. Adams
Mr. Attwater
Hon. Mrs. Arundell
Miss Arundell
   Attwater

B

Rev, Mr. Brown
   Benson
   Burch
Mr. Barfoot
   Ballard
   Biggs
   Beale
   Brownjohn
Mrs. Bearsley
   Boucher
   Best
   Blake

C

Mr. Crosield
   Curtoys
   Coster
   Carter
   Causway
Mrs. Clarke
   Cooper
   Corfe
   Crouch
Miss Chubb

D

Dr. Daniel
Mr. Dyke

Miss Dyker
   Davis

E

W. B. Earle, Esq.
Mr. Edgar, jun.
   Everett
   Elliott
Mrs. Edwards
Miss Edwards

F

Mr. Fiddes
   Freemantle
   H. Freke
   Forsyth
Mrs. Foster
Miss Fuller

G

Dr. Grove
Mr. Griesdale
   Goulden
   Green
Mrs. Goldwyre
   Gibbs
Miss Grubbe
   Goddard

H

Canon Hume
Rev. Mr. Holland
Colonel Hillman
Mr. Hawkins
   R. Hawkins
   Harris
Mrs. Hanham
   Hussey
   Hayter
   Hodding
   Hutfield
Miss Hawkins

J

Dr. Jacob
Mrs. Jeans

Mrs. Ivie
- Johnſon
Miſs Jacob
- Jukes

L

Mr. Long
- Lewis

M

Rev. Mr. Moore
Colonel Michel
Mr. Marſh
- J. Marſh
- D. Marſh
- Marks
- Merifield
- Mannings
Mrs. Martin
Miſs Moore

N

Mr. Newton
Mrs. Noel

O

Mr. Ogden

P

Francis Powell, Eſq.
Dr. Paul
Rev. Mr. Philips
Mrs. Pyke
Miſs Poore
- Prichards

R

Mr. Rolfe
Mrs. Ridding
- Rolleſtone
- Rothwell
- Rooke
- Richards
Miſs Reed
- Rendall

S

Nath. Still, Eſq. Mayor

Rev. Dr. Samber
Rev. Mr. Skinner
Mr. Shergold
- John Smith
- William Smith
- Sweatman
Mrs. Sympſon
- Sutton
- Slater
- Shuttleworth
- Sterne
Miſs Steele

T

William Trenchard, Eſq.
Mr. Tanner
- Thatcher

V

Mr. Vanderplank

W

Rev. Mr. Williams
Mr. Weſtcott
- Wyche
- White
- William Whitchurch
- Edmund White
- Wyatt
Mrs. Williams
- Wapſhare
- Wilkins
Miſs White
- Whitmarſh
- Weſtcott

ROMSEY.

CAPT. Wm. Brookman
- Mr. J. K. Comly
Mr. Thomas Hale
- J. Hedges
- Stephen Leach
- R. Newman

Rev.

Rev. Mr. Penton
Mr. Richard Pearce
    W. Sharp
Rev. Mr. Williams
Mr. Watts
    Waldron
Mrs. J. Forder
    H. Godfrey
    S. Hardyman
    Pain
    Wells
Miss Cock
    Fletcher
    Madgwick
    Moller
    Tarver
    Trodd
    Whiting

B A T H.

A
DUCHESS of Ancaster
    J. Akers, Esq. 3 Cop.
Rev. Mr. Armstrong
Mr. Anstley
    Arundell
    Atwood
    Abbott
Mrs. Astley
    S. Albyn

B
Hon. Henry Bennet
Capt. Blacker
Mr. Barry
    Thomas Beale
    Bond
    Browne
    Bryant
    Burges
    O. Bush

Lady Baynton
Mrs. Baker
    Battin
    Baldwin
    Bennet
    Bennet
    Bennett
    Boldwon
    Beale
    Bowdler
    Burge
    Burr
    Barry
    Buckworth
    Bell
    Bunney
Miss Brock
    Blacker

C
Lord Conyngham
Rev. Mr. Collins
Capt. Cooke
Mr. Collings
    Colborne
    Cadby
    Crawford
    Cruttwell
    Cullais
Mrs. Cunlieffe
    Colborne
    Cotes
    Cocknone
    Campbell
    Collett
    Carne
    Cracroft
    Crowe
    Caink
    Chapman
    Cowper
Miss Coker

Miss

Miſs Clutterbuck
Croſbie
Creſſwell

D

Dr. Dobſon
Wm. Davison, Eſq.
Mr. Dawſon
Mrs. Dawſon
Dunne
Dunne
Deane
Dory
Dawſon
Dimond
Dart
Miſs Dobree

E

Lady Erne
Rev. Mr. Elderton
Mr. Elliot
Mrs. Evans
Elton
Edwards
Miſs Enys

F

Lady Fetherſton
Dr. Falconer
Thomas Falconer, Eſq.
Mr. Franks
Mrs. Forbes
Forbes
Mrs. Fairfax
Forman
Miſs Falkner

G

Rev. Mr. Griffith
Gutteridge
Lady Glynn
Mrs. Glynn
Lady K. Gerald
Hon. Mrs. Grenville

Mrs. Gage
George
George
Gyde
Grimes
Miſs Greenwood

H

Counteſs of Howth
Lady Hervey
Hon. Mr. Hamilton
Col. Hunter
Rev. Mr. Hickes
Mr. Hagard
Hetwell
Harris
Harmer
Hepburn
Mrs. Holman
Haggitt
Hull
Holcombe
Harris
Hoare
Haward
Hawkins
Hetwell
Haſſard
Hancocke
Humphreys
Hedges
Henſhaw
Mrs. Hinxman
Miſs Hayward
Henton
Hallifan
Harriſon
Haſſall

J

Mr. James
Mrs. James
James

Mrs.

Mrs. Jackſon
Johnſon
Miſs Jackſon
Jones

K

Mr. Kilvert
King
Mrs. Krauter
Keaſberry
Miſs King

L

Lord Liſle
Lady Liſle
Mr. Lechmere
Lowfield
Mrs. H. Liſle
Linddiard
Lawford
Le Merchant
Lee
Le Meſurier
Miſs Leigh
Lewis

M

Lady Mannock
Hon. Mrs. Mackworth
Hon. Mrs. Moore
William Madden, Eſq.
Thomas Mead, Eſq.
Colonel Mackintoſh
Rev. Mr. Morgan
Mr. M. Martin
William Matthews
Mrs. Mackworth
Muniſon
Morgan
C. Morgan
Metholl
Martin
Morris
Melmoth

Mrs. Martyn
Moody
Mayler
Miſs Mendes
S. Mendes
Martin

N

Mrs. Negle
Newman
Needham
Miſs Newcome

O

Mrs. Onſlow
Miſs Owen

P

Gen. Parſlow
James Put
Mrs. Poole
Petty
Preſton
Peake
Porter
Procton
Miſs Pearce
Purlewent
Plunkett

R

Mr. Ruſſell
Rack
Mrs. Roſs
Roebuck
Robins
Miſs Rumbouilet

S

Lady Sydney
Stepney
Mary Stanley
Iſabella Stanley
Sir John Stapylton, Bart.
Dr. J. Smith
Dr. Staker

M

Mr. J. Symons
    Stroud
    Stracey
Mrs. Snee
    Savage
    Stone
    Stewart
    Saville
    Simpfon
    Smith
Mifs Stanley
    Swinburne
        T
Right Hon. Lady Tracy, 2 Copies
Capt. Tompfon
Mr. Thomfon
    Tully
    Townfend
    Timbrel, 2 Copies
Mrs. Thomfon
    Threfher, 2 Copies
    Torrent
    Trigg
    Toundrow

Mifs Tyler
    Torre
    Taylor
        V
Mrs. Vandewall
    Verker
        W
John Walcot, Efq.
Rev. Dr. Wilfon
Dr. Watfon
Mr. Wingrove
    Williams
    Wilfon
Mrs. Warwick
    Wheeller
    Welch
    Wignall
    White
    Wild
Mifs Waters
    Wrey
    Wiltfhire
    White
    Watts
    Wingrove

⁎ *It is hoped no Offence will be taken by any of the Subfcribers, fhould any of their Names be improperly fpelt, or their Titles of Diftinction omitted, as the Author had not the Honour of knowing many of them.*

THE
CONTENTS.

A   On

POEMS

POEMS

ON VARIOUS OCCASIONS.

The AUTHOR's PLEA.

WHO with a Critic's eye this book
        runs o'er,
Detects perhaps, a thousand faults, and more,
Impartially the Author's plea must hear,
And then perhaps will cease to be severe.

When reason first adorn'd my infant mind,
To books and poetry my heart inclin'd,

B   And

And as my years advanc'd, the passion
    grew,
And fair ideas round my fancy flew.
The Muses seem'd to court me for their
    friend,
But Fortune would not to their suit attend;
She understood who proper subjects were,
To hold a converse with these airy fair,
Must be possess'd at least of independence,
That to the Muses they may give at-
    tendance,
By books and study fructify the mind,
And lead the genius where it was inclin'd.
The inauspicious Dame deny'd that I,
Should thus, where Nature's self inclin'd,
    apply;
For she perceiv'd, I did the Muse befriend,
And could my days in contemplation spend,
                 Yet

Yet fo contracted, circumfcrib'd my line,
I paus'd—if to difcard the tuneful Nine.

Now duty calls my thoughts a different
    way;
Juftice enjoins; I muft her call obey.
So when the Mufes come on anxious wing,
Some pleafing fubject to my fancy, bring,
I bid them fly where peaceful leifure refts,
I have no time to entertain fuch guefts.
They oft affect a deafnefs, draw more near,
Declare that they can no repulfes bear,
Demand admittance, vow they are inclin'd,
To ftay till they imprint it on my mind.

Sometimes they are lefs bold, more fhyly
    come,
And with indiff'rence afk if I'm at home.

If duty will admit, I aſk them in,
When ſome engaging converſe they begin;
But ere, perhaps, the converſation's o'er,
Duty commands that we converſe no more.
Now Duty's call, I never muſt refuſe,
I riſe,—and with a bluſh myſelf excuſe;
Tell them I muſt withdraw a while, and
  when
Duty admits, I will return again.
Sometimes till I return, they deign to ſtay,
Sometimes they take offence, and fly
  away,
And never on that ſubject viſit more,
But bid me Fate's contracted hand deplore.

Thus, what the Author to the World
  preſents,
Appears through numberleſs impediments;
        And

And what of praife, or of difpraife you view,
To Nature and the Mufe is wholly due;
This, fhe prefumes, will candid minds
    fuffice,
And for her each defeat apologize.

On

On LOVE and WINE.

Written by Defire of P. G. Efq. of
WINCHESTER.

COME, defcend ye gentle Nine!
     Be Cupid too and Venus there;
When I fing of Love and Wine,
     Let Bacchus to my fong repair.

Love, of ev'ry theme the beft;
     Where this celeftial paffion reigns,
Oh! the houfe, the heart, how bleft,
     Silken bands are Hymen's chains!

Love will ev'ry fault conceal,
     And kindly each defect pafs o'er;
Generoufly each good reveal,
     And the minuteft grace explore.

Thofe

Thofe who wed for nought but gold,
    As well may marble rocks unite;
In their flinty cliffs enfold,
    And know Love's rapt'rous foft delight.

But when hands in wedlock join,
    And their twin'd hearts unite in Love;
Peace is their's, and joys divine,
    Next to thofe which reign above.

And fhould more aufpicious fate
    Beftow another bleffing ftill;
Deign our comforts to compleat,
    Our boards with Wine and Plenty fill.

Wine will chear the languid heart,
    And Love each angry thought controul
All that Nature afks, impart,
    And fill with Paradife the Soul.
                 Written

Written by the Defire of the Mifs B——s,
of WINCHESTER, on their parting with
Mr. and Mrs. G———N.

A H! gloomy, inaufpicious day,
     Which *tore* our charming friends
       away,
Which bids us from our G——N part,
And ftamps their abfence on our heart !
Let clouds and darknefs veil the fky,
And tears defcend from ev'ry eye.

    Adieu ye lovely happy pair,
Who all the focial comforts fhare ;
Love, joy, and calm tranquillity,
Compofe your bleft fociety.

                      With

With you what happy hours we've fpent,
In pleafure, mirth, and fweet content.
Alas! thofe pleafing days are o'er,
And you the B———s blefs no more.

But abfence fhall not damp our flame,
Friendfhip's pure lamp fhall burn the fame;
And while we have an ear to hear,
The name of G———n fhall be dear.

To

To a Young Gentleman, who presented
the Author with a Poem, in Commen-
dation of her Singing.

COULD I, arch youth, your flatt'ring
lines believe;
Were not your sex too subject to deceive,
I, like a credulous, unthinking maid,
Might be to thoughts of vanity betray'd ;
But, conscious my dull pipe no merit
claims,
My soul, like a stern oak, unmov'd re-
mains.

Were I assur'd that what those lines im-
part,
Was quite the genuine language of your
heart,

It

It furely would *demonftrate* a defect,
Which in my friend I wifh not to detect.
Your fenfe and judgment 'twould at once
    decry,
And prove you praife you know not what,
    nor why.
But I efteem your fenfe and penetration,
And thus conclude, from that confideration,
That all th' encomiums you on me beftow,
I, to your fkill in irony muft owe;
Your fex are quite proficients in this fchool,
And may elate the vain, unwary fool.

While I good-nature in my friend admire;
While grace and perfpicuity confpire,
To make him all a parent can defire,
Yet would I fay, as to the friend I love,
(For none fo good but he may ftill improve)
                 Would

Would you be thought a pleasing, hopeful
 youth,

Let all you write or speak be grac'd with
 truth.

Truth with resplendent lustre shews he
 face,

While falshood skulks, and sinks in black
 disgrace.

As you advance in years, in virtue grow,

So shall you her transcendant blessings know.

Virtue and Wisdom are entwined friends;

Who Virtue gains, true Wisdom appre-
 hends,

Heav'n guards his feet, and peace his
 steps attends.

Spoken

Spoken extempore to a young Lady, whofe
Name was ORGAN, on her Return Home,
after a few Months Abfence.

WHEN tuneful inftruments appear,
  They indicate fome pleafure near,
And if an Organ we behold,
It doth a facred theme unfold ;
It's one, it's chief, it's grand defign,
Is to break forth in fongs divine.
Welcome, fair inftrument of praife;
Thy prefence fhall our fpirits raife ;
And that thou art preferv'd from ill,
Art an unblemifh'd Organ ftill,
That ev'ry pipe's in tune, rejoice,
And we'll accord in heart and voice.

    C   THE

THE

WOMAN's ORNAMENT.

SYLVIA, as you defcend from line to
    line,
I know your judgment will concur with
    mine.
Should paffion with your better thoughts
    contend,
In Reafon's empire I've infur'd a friend.
While I attempt, tho' in a feeble ftrain,
My fexes brighteft ornament t' explain.

It centers not in yon unthinking lafs,
Who murders half her moments at the
    glafs.

That

That well dreſt cap, or better frizzled
    head,
With richeſt pearls and tow'ring plumes
    o'er-ſpread,
That lovely eaſy ſhape, or graceful air,
Which at the ball eclipſes all the fair;
That Angel's face, whoſe beauteous hues
    diſcloſe,
The ſnowy lilly, or the bluſhing roſe;
With iv'ry teeth, or more bewitching
    eyes,
Before whoſe luſtre ev'ry brilliant dies;
With voice harmonious, or enchanting
    tongue,
With pointed wit, or elocution hung;
With theſe, O Sylvia! you may be replete,
Yet want the pearl which makes you truly
    great.

B 2   But

But can you boaſt of wealth and ſtore of
    gold?
In you, ſome ſordid minds the gem behold;
Poſſeſt of this, you'll meet each ſwain's
    reſpeĉt,
It ſtrangely turns to beauty each defeĉt,
Makes prudence, virtue, ſenſe, and merit
    flow,
From ground where folly, vice, and malice
    grow.
But one eſteem'd the wiſeſt of the wiſe,
Beheld our ſexes worth with other eyes,
And her pronounces, of the pearl poſſeſt,
Who's with a meek and quiet ſpirit bleſt,
Whoſe ſoul retains ſound-judgment, ſolid
    ſenſe,
And virtue, with religion's noble fence;
An humble, gen'rous, free, exalted mind,
From all the groſſer ſentiments refin'd;

                     An

An heart fincere, fedate,—not apt to roam,
A mind domeftic, ever beft at home.
Be this my lot, my noble portion this,
And lo! I afk for no fuperior blifs.

CREDULIA's

CREDULIA's COMPLAINT.

A H! why thefe tears,—this rifing figh,
  Thefe foft impreffions yet;
Cannot fuch matchlefs perfidy
  Compel me to forget?

Ye rural walks, ye verdant meads,
  Ye folitary bowers,
Beneath your foft alluring fhades
  I've kill'd unnumber'd hours.

From you alone I feek redrefs,
  PERFIDIO's vows recal;
Perhaps you'll pity my diftrefs,
  For you have heard them all.

        Ah!

Ah ! with what tears did he invoke,
    What fighs my love implore,
A thoufand tender things he fpoke,
    And look'd a thoufand more.

Long did he feek CREDULIA's heart,
    Ere fhe that heart could give,
Till Cupid fhot that fatal dart,
    Which bade PERFIDIO live.

Now words were wanting to exprefs
    The tranfports of his foul,
He hop'd no more,—muft die with lefs,
    Her will fhould his controul.

Still more as with her converfe bleft,
    The gentle flame increas'd ;
'Twas Paradife within his breaft,
    When her his arms embrac'd.

                        And

And fhould fhe ever prove unkind,
　　Or with another wed,
He'd never change his ftedfaft mind,
　　But join the peaceful dead.

I heard nor did the fraud deteƈt,
　　The treach'rous fwain believ'd,
Nor once did my weak heart fufpeƈt,
　　I e'er fhould be deceiv'd.

But fuch I was;—Yet ftill the tear
　　Unwilling fills my eye,
And ftill I find his image there,
　　And ftill I heave a figh.

But rife, my foul, with juft difdain,
　　Regard the guilty youth,
Nor let him give thy bofom pain,
　　Who flies the path of truth.

　　　　　　　　　　　　On

On the Marriage of a LADY, to whom the
Author was Bride-Maid.

AS the light bark on the tempeftuous fea,
  Tofs'd to and fro, from dangers never
   free;
Difmay'd with fear, and mov'd with ev'ry
  blaft,
Till in a port her anchor's firmly caft;
So oft is mov'd Man's fluctuating mind,
Till it in wedlock a fafe anchor find;
Here, if the foul but meets her deftin'd
  mate,
Her joys are full, her happinefs compleat.

 Be this your happy lot, my lovely friend,
Whofe nuptial rites I this glad morn
  attend;
         Whofe

Whofe humble, gentle mind for peace was
     born,

Whom virtue, love, and innocence adorn.

Celeſtial graces dignify thy ſoul,

While pure religion all thy ways controul.

Theſe noble virtues, which in thee abound,

Are haply in thy lov'd PHILANDER
     found.

His heart ſincere, his temper ſoft and
     mild,

Nor torn by anger, nor with art beguil'd.

Such gentle hearts alone ſhould join their
     hands,

And find that Hymen's chains are ſilken
     bands.

Their emulation's not who'll reign ſu-
     preme,

But who ſhall love the moſt,—be moſt
     ſerene.

                        Remote

Remote from vanity and wordly toys,
Each feeks with each for more fubftantial
    joys.
Tranquillity fhall in their borders dwell,
Nor difcord once approach their peaceful
    cell,
But mutually each other's grief they'll bear,
As mutually each other's joys will fhare.

Thus, thus, my friend, may you for
    ever prove,
The foft delight of harmony and love;
May ev'ry blelling you can afk of Heav'n,
To conftitute your happinefs be giv'n.
If Heav'n beftows, with joy receive the
    prize,
If Heav'n witholds, 'tis beft what Heav'n
    denies.

                    Thus

Thus fweetly may you pafs your future
        life,
Nor once repent that you became a wife;
That you declin'd the pleafing name of
        B——m,
And that alone preferr'd of H——rag—m.

From

From EUSEBIA to FIDELIO.

ERE you, FIDELIO, thefe foft lines
  fhall view,
We fhall have fpoke that painful word,
  Adieu!
I know the anguifh of your faithful heart,
I know you thought it more than death to
  part;
But now 'tis done;—The dreaded trial's
  o'er,
Your lov'd EUSEBIA you behold no more.
No more on willing feet together walk,
Or of our joys, or of our forrows talk;
When each, as to a friend fincere and kind,
Difclos'd the fond emotions of the mind.

    D   No

No more FIDELIO's arms become my bed,

Or on his neck reclines my drooping head

Days, weeks, and months muſt in ſucceſſion
  glide,

Ere you, again, will join EUSEBIA's ſide.

O'er hills and dales ſhe takes her diſtant
  flight,

And mountain tops obſcure her from your
  ſight;

Long lanes, and fields, and meadows
  cloath'd in green,

And many a weary ſtep, lies now between.

Perhaps, ere this, a tear bedews your eye,

And your ſad boſom heaves a tender ſigh;

But ſpare your tears, of this your heart
  aſſure,

Mine eyes enough for you and I procure.

         So

So let no doubts your conftant heart affail,
For none but you, FIDELIO, fhall prevail:
Shou'd Heav'n advance me to the higheft
      fphere,
You only are, and ever fhall be dear.
That gen'rous heart, which fought not
      gold, but me,
Shall meet its equal, noble, gen'rous, free.
Fair Fortune fmiles and I'll again return,
And bid my juft FIDELIO ceafe to mourn.
Our conftant hearts, our willing hands fhall
      join,
Thy lov'd EUSEBIA fhall be wholly thine.
But if on earth we ne'er fhall meet again,
In this afflictive world of grief and pain;
If Heav'n, all-wife, erects my nuptial
      bed,
Within the peaceful regions of the dead,

I hope to meet you in that world above,,

Where it will be adjudg'd no crime to
　　　love;

Where *fathers* cannot frown, nor friends
　　　difmay,

But all be joy through one eternal day.

On

On the Marriage of Captain A—— to Miſs R——.

Y E Nymphs of Helicon, attend my
      lyre,
While all the feather'd Choriſters conſpire,
In notes celeſtial to ſalute the morn,
When SYLVIA doth the nuptial rites adorn.
See Cupids, Sylphs, and Goddeſſes deſcend;
Venus and all her gentle train attend;
While ev'ry fragrant flow'r appears in
      bloom,
And minds moſt penſive diſſipate their
      gloom.
All happy in this nuptial joy to ſhare,
And each congratulates the happy pair.

The

The happy pair, who, lock'd in Hymen's
     bands,
United hearts, ere they united hands.

Orenzo's heart, to martial fields enur'd,
Who all the hoftile acts of war endur'd,
One tender look from Sylvia quite dif-
     arms;
But where's the bofom can withftand fuch
     charms?
When beauty, grace, and innocence com-
     bin'd,
T' infpire the foul, and captivate the mind.
Who proof remains, 'gainft cannon balls
     and fire,
May by one glance from Sylvia's eyes
     expire.
Thofe lovely eyes emitted fuch a dart,
As made a conqueft of Orenzo's heart;

A noble conqueſt, worthy of the fair,
Who in his future joys and grief will ſhare.

How bleſt the ſwain, of ſuch a bride
    poſſeſt !
The nymph ally'd to ſuch a ſwain, how
    bleſt !
Long may you live,—connubial life adorn ;
Yea, live to bleſs the children yet unborn,
Live,—and no other emulation know,
But who the greateſt tenderneſs ſhall ſhew ;
And when fair SYLVIA feels a Mother's care
May ſhe a Mother's conſolation ſhare ;
May ev'ry tender branch that ſhall be giv'n,
Be fructify'd with all the gifts of Heav'n.
While SYLVIA, who by good example's
    taught,
Whoſe mind is by maternal wiſdom
    fraught,
                    With

With such inftruction, as purfu'd through
    life,
Will grace the mother, and adorn the wife.
Fair SYLVIA will, with notions moft refin'd,
Direct their fteps, and cultivate the mind.
ORENZO too, with a paternal heart,
Will all that's ufeful, kind, or good,
    impart.
Thus, with each joy, and focial comfort
    bleft,
Each morn they'll rife, and eve retire to reft.

Should duty, loyalty, or war's alarms,
Demand ORENZO from his SYLVIA's arms,
With rage redoubl'd, he'll engage the foe,
And fink them fwiftly down to fhades
    below;
Bid each the fatal confequences prove,
Who dares detain the hero from his love.

                      Thus

Thus conqu'ring more by Cupid than by
   Mars,
Fly to his fair triumphant from the wars;
Find in her virtuous arms that fweet repaft,
Which lawlefs libertines can never tafte;
Her ev'ry look fhall joys fublime create,
And make a Paradife of his retreat.

A

A

LETTER to an AUNT.

DEAR Madam pleafe to pardon me,
 That I with you this freedom take,
But thus a kind enquiry,
 After your health is all I make.

My parents, felf, and fifters too,
 Thro' mercy are extremely well;
And hope, and long, and pray that you,
 This pleafing news may have to tell.

Alas ! tis more than fix long years,
 Since you and I were forc'd to part,
I need not tell, for fure my tears
 Confefs'd how much it mov'd my heart.

       This

This penfive thought my mind impreft,
    Alas ! I ne'er fhall fee her more ;
Then was my fpirit fo diftreft,
    That fill'd with grief, my eyes ran o'er.

And now again, with grief I fay,
    I ne'er expect your face to fee,
Since nothing calls me hence your way,
    And nothing calls you thence to me.

But if we never meet below,
    While we thefe mortal bodies wear,
When you, dear Aunt, to Heav'n fhall go,
    May 1 be bleft to meet you there.

While yet appears your fetting fun,
    Some fleeting moments yet remain ;
If ev'ry family fhould be one,
    Why may not ink our paper ftain.

                            Madam,

Madam, if you will condefcend
 To write, if but a fingle line,
You'll much oblige your loving friend,
 An humble fav'rite of the Nine.

But fhould I not this favour gain,
 Till Death tranfmits me to my grave,
I wifh, dear Madam, to remain,
 Your loving dutious niece, JANE CAVE.

On

On the Departure of a Youth from the
Author, with whom fhe had lived near
two Years.

D AYS, weeks, and months are gone
and paft,
This morning ufhers in the laft,
The laft,—that ever we, my friend,
May in one habitation fpend.
But ere we part, my friendly mufe
Wou'd kindly this precaution ufe.

You now are juft in manhood's dawn,
And flow'ry profpects deck the lawn;
Wealth, pleafure, ftrength, and length of
days,
With joyful hope, your mind furveys.

E   But

But let your heart receive this truth,
Ten thoufand fnares are laid for youth;
Ten thoufand fins, in pleafure's drefs,
Each youth will to their bofom prefs.
One fin calls here, another there,
And youth, too oft, incline an ear,
The foft delufive voice to hear.

Regard then this my parting breath,
Thofe flow'ry paths lead down to death,
And when you are from me remote,
With gay companions, void of thought;
When you fhall hear their tongues profane
The great JEHOVAH's facred name,
And you, perhaps, with them fhall join
To imprecate the wrath divine,
Tho' no reproving friend is near,
Remember God himfelf is there.

Let

Let recollection then relate,
What oft you've heard a friend repeat,
Confcience fhall ev'ry truth atteft,
And own each admonition juft;
She will a faithful diary keep,
Tho' oft we think fhe's lull'd to fleep.
But ah !—fhould death your foul o'ertake,
You'd find the treach'rous dame awake;
But this obfcure, this laft fad day,
Youth fhuns, and puts it far away.
But come, or foon, or late that hour,
We know we all muft feel its pow'r.

This long expected period's come,
As certain *that*, which feals our doom,
Which ftabs our vitals,—draws our breath,
And clofes up our eyes in death,
Which makes us bid the world Adieu !
And brings eternity to view,

Which

Which hails us partners of the fky,
Or bids us down to horror fly :
Then fhall your heart thefe lines approve,
And know that all I meant was love.

Written to a Friend, on going to ITCHEN,
about five Miles from WINCHESTER, to
fee a Country Seat belonging to the Duke
of Chandos.

A Friendly party, of one mind,
Were for a pleafure-day inclin'd,
Forfook their beds on Thurfday morn,
When each their perfons did adorn

With

With raiment proper for the day,
And in high fpirits drove away.

   The morn did a bad day portend,
Bid fome unwelcome fhow'rs defcend;
But fable clouds now difappear,
And azure decks the atmofphere;
Phœbus expands his golden rays,
And all the rural fweets difplays,
And that my friend the whole may know,
We to a place call'd ITCHEN go;
Where, with an honeft batchelor,
We meet with good and hearty cheer.
Sincere, ingenuous, plain and free,
No needlefs compliment had he.
Each welcome, what he lik'd to chufe,
And each as welcome to refufe.
A while we after dinner fat,
Engag'd in inoffenfive chat,

E 3

Then

Then arm in arm, in pairs we ftalk,
And to his Grace's manfion walk.
Here, each apartment we behold,
Doth fomething of the Duke unfold.
Magnificence decks ev'ry place,
And fpeaks the owner is his Grace.
Some ancient portraits caught my eye,
Which bid my bofom heave a figh,
For ah! thofe once lov'd forms with
     reptiles lie.

When we had view'd the manfion o'er,
Park, garden, fifh-ponds, and much more,
Our feeble frames begin to tire,
And fome refrefhment we require.
We now approach the humble cell,
Wherein our ruftic friend doth dwell.
Here, fill'd with new ideas, we
Regale us with a difh of tea.

                           Some

Some hours yet remain unſpent,
And pleaſure was our ſole intent.
So that we may the ſame increaſe,
Reſolv'd the chryſtal ſtream to trace,
Forthwith into a boat we go,
And up and down the river row,
See the glad fiſhes friſk and play,
And ſeem as bleſt, and pleas'd as they.

Re-ent'ring now our friends retreat,
To make his bounty quite compleat,
A pleaſant ſyllabub we find,
When each may drink, who is inclin'd.

Phœbus now haſtens to the weſt,
We think to haſten home is beſt;
So parting with our gen'rous friend,
Wiſhing each bliſs may him attend,
Enter our carriage, drive away,
Beſtow encomiums on the day.

None

None feem'd inclining to relent,
Each had a day of pleafure fpent;
Thus chatting on, till we alight,
And bid each other a good night.

Thankful, we all are fafe and well,
And that no ill has us befel;
Each to their dwelling go their way,
And thus concludes our pleafure-day.

A Poem, occafioned by a Lady's doubting
whether the Author compofed an Elegy,
to which her Name is affix'd.

IF good Mifs H— will condefcend,
    To read thefe lines which I have penn'd,
Perhaps it may her doubts confute,
And fhe'll no more my word difpute,
                                      But

But own I may the Author be,
Of what ſhe did on Sunday ſee.

  You'd hate a baſe perfidious youth,
Such *my* diſguſt to all untruth.
A gen'rous mind is never prone,
To claim a merit not her own.
I wou'd diſdain t' affix my name
To that, which is another's claim.
Of beauteous form Heav'n made me not,
(Nor has ſore affluence been my lot,)
But fix'd me in an humble ſtation,
Remote from thoſe of rank and faſhion;
But there are beauties of the mind,
Which are not to the great confin'd;
Wiſdom does not erect her ſeat
Always in palaces of ſtate;
This bleſſing Heav'n diſpenſes round,
She's ſometimes in a cottage found,

                  And

And tho' ſhe is a gueſt majeſtic,
May deign to dwell in a domeſtic.

Yet, of this great celeſtial gueſt,
I dare not boaſt myſelf poſſeſt,
But this wou'd repreſent to you,
As Wiſdom does, the Muſes do,
No def'rence ſhew to wealth or eaſe,
But pay their viſits as they pleaſe.
Sometimes they deign to call on me,
And tune my mind to poetry :
But all : they're fled, I'll drop my pen,
Nor raiſe it till they call again.

A

A POEM for CHILDREN.

On Cruelty to the Irrational Creation.

OH! what a cruel wicked thing,
    For me who am a little King, *
To give my haplefs fubjects pain,
And make them groan beneath my reign.

Were I a chafer, and could fly,
Ah! fhould I not with anguifh cry,
Should naughty children take a pin,
And run me through to make me fpin?

Were I a bird, took from my neft,
Should I not think myfelf oppreft,
If tofs'd about in wanton play,
'Till maim'd and faint I die away?

* See PSALMS, viii. vi.

                            No

Now, and when I'm a bigger boy,
Let cruelty my heart annoy,
Becaufe it is a dreadful evil,
That only fits me for the Devil.

If I muft ought of life deprive,
The quickeft way I will contrive,
To ftop the tremb'ling victim's breath,
And give it little pain in death.

I'll not torment a dog or cat;
A toad, a viper, or a rat;
They're form'd by an Almighty hand,
And fprung to life at his command.

A bull, a horfe, yea every creature,
Of the moft mild or favage nature,
Were kindly given for my ufe,
But never meant for my abufe.

Good

Good men, thy holy word attefts,
Are kind and tender to their beafts;
May I be merciful and kind,
That I with thee may mercy find.

Written by Defire of a Lady, on an angry,
petulant Kitchen-Maid.

GOOD Miftrefs Difhclout, what's the
matter?
Why here—the fpoon, and there—the
platter?
What demon caufes all this low'ring,
Black as the pot you oft are fcow'ring?
Hot as the fire you daily light,
Your fpeech with low invectives blight,

F   While

While rage impregnates ev'ry vein,
And dies the face *one crimfon ftain.*

   Sure fome one has a word mifplac'd,
Or look'd not equal to your tafte,
Or, is this juft the time you've chofe,
Your great acquirements to difclofe,
Difplay the graces of your tongue,
Shew with what eloquence 'tis hung,
As dog, rogue, fcoundrel, fcrub, what not,
And twenty more, I've quite forgot;
Which prove to a demonftration
You've had a liberal education;
Such titles muft enchant the ear,
And make the bounteous donor dear;
But while thefe bounties are difpenfing,
I wifh I'd learn'd the art of fencing,
Leaft while at John you aim to throw,
My nob fhould chance to catch the blow;

                       Then

Then I fhould get a broken pate,
And marks of violence I hate.

 Good Miftrefs Difhclout condefcend
To hear the counfel of a friend;
When next you are difpos'd to brawl,
Pray let the fcull'ry hear it all,
And learn to know, your fitteft place
Is with the difhes and the greafe,
And when you are inclin'd to battle,
Engage the fkimmer, fpit, or kettle,
Or any other kitchen gueft,
Which you in wifdom might think beft..

Written

Written by Defire of a Mother, who had
    loft an only Child.

A S with delight we view the op'ning
       rofe
Expand, and all her fragrant fweets difclofe,
So did MATERNA view her lovely maid,
In all the charms of innocence array'd;
Oft had her little all, her only child,
The tedious hour with pleafing chat be-
      guil'd,
But Heav'n, all-good, and infinitely wife,
Remov'd this darling idol to the fkies,
Ere her young heart had been *obdur'd* by fin,
Or guilt, tormenting fiend, could brood
      therein,
Ere fhe arriv'd at years that might deftroy,
By one falfe ftep, a tender mother's joy.
                Behold

Behold fhe foars to yon celeftial fields,
Where ev'ry plant æthereal odour yields;
With pitying eye, methinks fhe looks below,
Commifferates a tender mother's woe,
Bids her dejected heart from earth retire,
And all her future thoughts to Heav'n
     afpire;
Prepare, fhe cries,—prepare to meet the
     bleft,
And join your SALLY in eternal reft.

On the Author's leaving BATH and going to
WINCHESTER, Nov. 13, 1779.

ALAS! 'tis done, I can no longer ftay,
    For Tuefday morn will hurry me
    away

From BATH,—from friends whofe friend-
  fhip I revere,
Friends—moft difint'refted and fincere ;
I bid them all adieu ! and go alone,
To a ftrange place, unknowing and un-
  known.
I know your kindeft wifhes me attend,
And in this place may raife to me a friend.

 I go,—but fome, alas! from whom I
  part,
Like a kind parent lie within my heart,
And cou'd I know we part, to meet no more,
I wou'd each thought of parting now give
  o'er.

 My tears prevent,—why do mine eyes
  o'erflow,
And why my heart fuch poignant forrow
  know ?

       But

But can I,—dare I, unaffected be,
With such unmerited respect to me ?
I nought possess, I nothing can return,
But sure my heart with gratitude shall burn ;
Indelible *their* kindness shall remain,
Nor will I wish my passions to restrain.

My pray'rs and tears (would they were
      prevalent !)
Shall be to Heav'n by ardent breathing
      sent,
That ev'ry wish'd for blessing may descend
On each whom kindness constitutes my
      friend ;
May plenty, life, and health with each
      remain,
And I be blest to meet you all again.

But should pale Death for either of you
      call,
Or fix on me, and force me from you all,

                                        Be

Be this my pray'r, till my frail life is o'er,
That we may meet on yon celeftial fhore,
Where death, and grief, and parting are
    no more.

A Poem, on the Celebration of the Night
  in which Miffes W——— and J——— were
 bound Apprentices to Mifs H. of Bath.

IN love and innocent delight
   We meet to fpend this wifh'd for night;
When FLAVIA and SELIME are bound;
And may their time with peace be crown'd.
May health and harmony, and love,
And all the bleffings from above,
Crown ev'ry day kind Heav'n fhall give,
Whilft you fhall with fair SILVIA live.

                May

May FLAVIA, and young SELIME too,
(As friends confiſtently may do)
In this each other emulate,
Who ſhall with knowledge be replete;
Who be moſt active, moſt ſincere,
Who moſt in goodneſs perſevere:
And whilſt fair SILVIA rules with eaſe,
Be your ambition ſtill to pleaſe.
So peace ſhall crown your fleeting hours,
Content and happineſs be yours.

Written by the Deſire of a Lady, On Build-
ing of Caſtles.

BUILDING of Caſtles did commence,
In days of old, for our defence,
And uſually erected were,
Adjacent to the Seat of war;

Where

Where blood and flaughter did abound,
And drench'd with gore the thirfty ground;
Where powder, darts, and bullets flew,
Nor one relenting paffion knew;
But winging through the fmoke and fire,
Made thoufands groan, bleed, and expire.

Caftles were built firm and fecure,
Wherein fome treafure to infure;
With cells and caverns dark, profound,
And walls impregnable around.
It's direful decorations are
The whole artillery of war;
Cannons and mufkets, fwords and bombs,
Hangers and fpears, and fifes and drums.
Bullets, and ev'ry fit fupply,
Wherewith t'attack the enemy.

Some caftles too, of which we hear,
Are fabricated in the air;

But

But thefe are of the mental kind,
The fole conftruction of the mind.
We in thefe æther caftles ride,
With all the equipage of pride,
And in imagination rife,
Superior monarchs of the fkies.
One blaft this edifice deftroys,
Abortive are our promis'd joys.
Our miniftry this caftle built,
By which the blood of thoufands fpilt;
Fancy'd a thoufand men or two
Could all AMERICA fubdue.
But thrice ten thoufand crofs'd the main,
A million's in the conteft flain.
Yet, ah! fell caftle, direful ill,
AMERICA's un-conqu'red ftill.

    Caftles are an imperfect plan,
Of that fuperior creature,—Man.

The

The body is a caftle where,

The moft intrinfic treafures are;

Well fraught with arms for man's defence

As reafon, recollection, fenfe;

Which if we exercife aright,

Put all our Enemies to flight;

Spoil Envy with her pois'nous dart,

And wound Refentment to the heart;

Bid Difcontent and Anger fly,

And each unruly paffion die;

Subdue Diftruft and b!ack Defpair,

And fubftitute Contentment there.

Thus conqu'ring, we fuperior rife

With fhouts of vict'ry to the fkies.

Where ev'ry Conqueror is bleft,

In Caftles of eternal reft.

The

The AUTHOR perfonates the MOTHER
viewing the Portrait of Mr. T. W. who
was then in the EAST INDIES.

L O! here the lovely portrait's feen,
   But, ah! what oceans roll between;
What tracks of land, and deferts wild,
Divide me from my darling child!
Carnage, and Death triumphant reign,
Storms rife, and thunders roar in vain,
Nor rocks, nor racks, nor wars deter,
The dear, the bold Adventurer;
Difdaining affluence, peace, and eafe,
He braves the horrors of the feas.
   Thou, whofe omnifcient eye-pervades
Celeftial heights, and darkeft fhades,
Surveys at once each point of land,
And holds the ocean in thy hand,

G   Preferve

Preferve this brave advent'rous youth,
And lead him to the paths of truth;
Still o'er his ev'ry thought prefide,
And bid his foul in thee confide.
Preferve him, till each danger's o'er,
And land him on his native fhore;
Then our exulting hearts fhall raife
A fong of gratitude and praife.

Written to an Aunt, accompanied with
Two Elegies.

MADAM, your Niece refumes her pen,
    And writes to her dear Aunt again;
That you may fee her weak attempts,
Humbly two Elegies prefents.
Begs you will kindly them accept
With this precaution—don't expect

                                    Any

Any great worth in them to fee,
For they were wholly made by me.
Tho' quite imperfect, don't refufe
The labours of a Female's Mufe,
But kindly each defect pafs o'er,
Your niece JANE CAVE will afk no more.

On feeing Lady P— at a Place of Worfhip.

MY flighted Mufe long time had flown,
    And great difguft to me had fhewn;
But yefterday fhe call'd again,
And forc'd me to refume my pen.
   " Behold! fhe faid, yon lovely face,
" Which Nature form'd with fo much grace,
" Riches and honours are her own,
" And focial comforts yet unknown,
" Prudence, that lov'd tho' humble gueft,
" Erects a throne within her breaft.

G 2   " When

" When plac'd within the Houfe of Pray'r,

" She recollected GOD was there;

" Tho' Levity was by her fide,

" She with a fweet becoming pride,

" Rebuk'd the fair——devoutly fat,

" Nor once prefum'd to laugh or chat:

" For well fhe knew 'twould fink her down

" Below the level of a Clown.

" That titles only agrandize,

" And bid us as fuperiors rife,

" In juft proportion as they're join'd,

" Unto a great ennobled mind;

" Who, with a proper, humble grace,

" Demeans herfelf in ev'ry place,

" Such is the fair of whom I fpeak,

" For whom I did this vifit make."

Thus fpake my Mufe, then took her flight

In æther, and out foar'd my fight.

POEMS

POEMS
SACRED TO THE
MEMORY of the DEAD.

On the Death of Mr. BRADFORD, an eminent Gardener in BRISTOL, July, 1774.

WHERE are thofe wonted feet, O tell
  me where!
That to this garden did fo oft repair ?
Behold! I fearch, but ah! I fearch in vain,
Alas! no traces of them here remain.
 Ye plants and flow'rs, come tell me if
  you can,
Where is the good, laborious, faithful man,

G 3

Who

Who daily view'd you with discerning
      eye,
Wou'd ev'ry beauty, ev'ry fault espy?
Nect'rines and peaches, apricots and all
Ye pleasant fruits, that are within my call,
Where are those hands, that with an artful
      care
Oft prun'd your trees, knew when to prune,
      and where?
Hot-house and green-house, next I ask of
      you,
But ye unwilling are to tell me too.
Of ev'ry plant, and tree, and flow'r I ask,
But none will undertake the painful task,
The truly fatal, pensive news to tell,
To say their friend has took his long
      farewel,
For all his loss, in silent grief deplore,

                  Their

Their looks proclaim that BRADFORD is no
    more.

No more, methinks they fay, we fee our
    friend,

Who weeks, and months, and years with
    us did fpend;

Who planted us, and fet us firft to grow,

Tranfplanted us, and mov'd us to and fro.

Us to improve, was BRADFORD's chief de-
    light,

His work by day, and ftudy too by
    night.

Before the rifing of yon radient fun,

Each morn our friend his daily work begun.

Yea, oft with fair Aurora he would rife,

For us the foft alluring bed defpife.

Now no fuch care and conftancy we find,

Alas! his equal is not left behind.

                       Whilft

Whilft thus the penfive flow'rs his worth
    repeat,
The plants and trees their cries reverberate:
And I'll their authenticity atteft,
His worth and merit were by all confeft,
He was labor'ous, careful, wife, and good,
Each plant and tree minutely underftood.
He was,—but ah! I'll not recount his praife,
'Twill not allay our grief, but forrow raife;
For now he is no more, but borne away,
From realms of forrow to celeftial day.
Propitious Heav'n beheld, and mov'd with
    love
Kindly remov'd him hence to realms above,
And when he found his diffolution nigh,
He faid, " Come, wife, fit down, and fee
    me die."
Serene and calm he bow'd his peaceful head,
Without a groan the willing fpirit fled.
                  And

And when this tranſitory life is o'er,
O may his partner gain the happy ſhore,
Triumphant in a flaming car aſcend,
And ever dwell with her departed friend !

On the Death of Mrs. MAYBERY, of BRECON.

AND can it be ? and is her ſpirit fled ?
    Is dear OPHELIA number'd with the
    dead ?
Are all the days of her probation paſt ?
And is her die unalterably caſt ?
Heart piercing thought—flow tears from
    ev'ry eye,
While ev'ry boſom, riſes with a ſigh.
What goodneſs, prudence, wiſdom, laid in
    duſt !
Ah ! Who the greateſt Potentate can truſt !
                         Where

Where's he ! could I each mortal's name
     rehearfe,
Who pow'r hath gain'd this fentence to
     reverfe.

Obdurate King—Infatiable Death !
Who thus a period puts to mortals breath;
By thy rude hand no defference is paid,
Greatnefs with indigence in duft is laid;
Deftruction is effential to thy name,
And all thy direful acts thy pow'r pro-
     claim.
What hopes are fpoil'd ? What near con-
     nections broke,
By this thy fudden unrelenting ftroke?
The life deftroy'd, the valuable life
Of miftrefs, fifter, daughter, mother, wife.

  See her domeftics who her goodnefs knew,
Pour forth the tribute to her merit due,
               While

While weeping fifters bath'd in tears remain,
And fighing brothers fcarce their grief
   fuftain.
While tender, aged Parents' hearts o'erflow,
Nor joy nor reft, nor confolation know,
While duteous children, fent her by the Lord,
In fruitlefs tears the mournful day record.
And then behold, but ah ! what heart can
   guefs
The grief profound, the depth of that diftrefs,
Which feiz'd at once the partner of her bed,
When told his wife, his other felf was dead ?
Trembling methinks, with ev'ry thought
   amaz'd,
Aftonifh'd at the meffenger he gaz'd !
The vital ftream congeals in ev'ry vein,
While fcarcely fpirits, ftrength, or life
   remain.

       Anxious

Anxious at once 'the whole dread fcene to
   know,
Yet dreads to hear what will increafe his woe.
At length inform'd—delug'd in grief he lies,
Nor hopes redrefs, but from his weeping eyes.
He calls the friendly tear to eafe his grief,
But thefe recoil, nor deign to give relief.
Thus with an heart o'erbórne, and fpirits
   broke,
He finks beneath th'intolerable ftroke.
He ruminates—at length the filence breaks,
And thus methinks, in penfive accents fpeaks;
Alas! for me, my happier days are o'er,
I hear the voice—behold the face no more
Of her my friend, my beft belov'd, my wife,
The joy, fupport, and comfort of my life;
The tender mother of my progeny,
The prudent miftrefs of my family;

      How

How many ufeful years might fhe have
    fpent,
To blefs thofe children, which by Heav'n
    are lent,
To guide their feet, inculcate filial fear,
While ev'ry look maternal love did bear ?
Her care judicioufly, rul'd all within,
When I, for weeks and months have abfent
    been.
My help-mate fhe, who with fuperior grace,
Adorn'd the miftrefs, wife, and mother's
    place.
Thus mourns her fpoufe, while numbers
    fwell the cry,
Her death demands a tear from ev'ry eye.
In her the poor and wretched found a friend,
On her did for their chief fupport depend.
Bleft with a noble, free, and gen'rous heart,
In her mean av'rice could claim no part.

        H   And

And now 'twould be but juft, if in return
A flood of tears were pour'd upon her urn :
While all thofe grievances fhe did redrefs,
Her name and memory for ever blefs.

On the Death of Mrs. BLAKE, of Crock-
    horn, who died in a Week after being
    fafely delivered of the fixth Child.

WHAT eye forbids a tear, what heart
        a figh ?
Fly fome aufpicious Angel, quickly fly !
The ftroke is too fevere for man to bear,
If fome celeftial comfort be not there.

How anxioufly the lov'd Eusebius ftands,
To Heav'n in pray'r lifts up his ardent
        hands,
That when the trying period fhall arrive,
The dear Amata be preferv'd alive.
                                    At

At length the hour advances, Heav'n feems
 kind,
And lo! a lovely infant foon we find;
The dear maternal friend bids fair for life,
And the fond hufband views his lovely wife,
The living mother of a living child;
And all the hufband all the father fmil'd;
Joy fills his heart, love fparkles in his eyes,
And each foreboding thought before him dies.
His grateful heart afcends in praife to Heav'n,
Whofe goodnefs had this double blefling giv'n.
Each friend congratulates the happy pair,
And wifhes in their mutual joy to fhare.
Life fmiles on all, no trouble feems t'annoy,
But ah! fad change—How tranfient is the
 joy?
Each heart where gladnefs fat—beneath the
 ftroke
Sinks to defpair, and all it's comfort's broke.

Her

Her face, which yielded pleafure and delight,
At once turns pale and folemn as the night;
Gloom fpreads around, her Sun withdraws
   his rays,
And fets in the meridian of her days.
She meekly yields, finks from the fondeft
   arms,
She dies!—and with her die a thoufand
   charms;
  In her the moft endearing wife is dead,
The tend'reft mother from her children fled:
The courteous neighbour, faithful friend
   fhe prov'd,
In life by all refpected and belov'd,
By all lamented when from life remov'd.
Earth feem'd unworthy of her longer ftay,
And Heav'n receiv'd her to celeftial day;
There fhe beholds the glories of her Lord,
And all her virtues meet a full reward.
        On

On the Much Lamented DEATH of the
Rev. Mr. WHITFIELD, who died in
NEW ENGLAND, Sept. 30, 1770.

WHY doth all Nature wear an awful
        gloom?
And why, alas! exults yon diftant tomb?
Why doth a fable cloud the fky o'er-fpread?
WHITFIELD alas! feraphic WHITFIELD's
        dead,
The Friend, the Chriftian, the approv'd
        Divine,
The Saint in whom the life of GOD did fhine,
The man whom Heav'n ordain'd to preach
        for all,
And thoufands by his miniftry to call;
The Lord did chufe him in his youthful
        days,
To fpeak his glory and fet forth his praife.

     H 3   Mov'd

Mov'd by celeftial love, did undertake,
The miniftry alone for JESU's fake.
His tongue was touch'd with evangelic fire,
And heav'nly raptures did his foul infpire.
Then forth into the World this Herald came,
Refolv'd to propagate IMMANUEL's name ;
To fet his glory forth from pole to pole,
Were the capacious breathings of his foul.
He loudly did the Gofpel trumpet found,
Whilft thoufands trembl'd as they ftood
      around,
Proclaim'd the fuff'rings of a dying GOD,
Invited finners to his pard'ning blood,
Enforc'd to all the great neceffity
Of knowing this—" The Saviour dy'd for
      me."
Thus was our nation blefs'd with Gofpel
      truth,
Boldly deliver'd by this chofen Youth,
                              Who

Who with an heart inflam'd with JESU's love,
Caus'd GOD to pour his bleffings from above.
But did this Champion for the living GOD,
Appear in England only, to do good ?
No, no, his gracious Captain points his way
Beyond the feas, and Whitfield muft obey :
For in his Maker's will he did rejoice,
Was all attention to his facred voice.
When JESUS bade o'er raging feas to pafs,
Through vaft AMERICA, to found his grace,
There, like an Herald for the bleeding
   Lamb,
He went, and did the Negroes fouls inflame.
Shew'd Ethiopians their Redeemer nigh,
To cleanfe their fpotted fouls from deepeft
   dye.
In fuch pathetic accents mov'd his tongue,
As rent and broke the very heart of ftone.
       Thus

Thus did he found his Maker's praife abroad,

A lab'rer in the vineyard of his GOD.

But now, alas! his labours are all o'er,

The fields do eccho with his voice no more;

No more from his dear Englifh friends he

      parts,

No more returns to animate their hearts,

But leaves ten thoufand thoufands to deplore

The death of him, who lives to die no more.

Let things inanimate his worth proclaim!

And fhout from fea to fea his wond'rous

      name!

O ye nocturnal luminaries tell,

What love for fouls did in his bofom dwell!

Say, fay what nights this advocate with

      GOD

Spent wreftling to avert th'impending rod.

Let fair AURORA in her turn declare,

How he preceded her by praife and pray'r.

                 Let

Let churches, chapels, tabernacles tell,
Who e'er within their walls did him excel.
Let counties, cities, towns, and ftreets pro-
    claim,
How faithfully he did the truth maintain.
Say winds and waves, how oft the Saint ye
    tofs'd,
When he for God the great Atlantic crofs'd ?
And let the Continent abroad begin,
To tell what heav'nly news he there did
    bring,
How he explain'd the love of Jesu's heart,
'Till finners with their ev'ry fin did part.
Hell trembl'd when this god=like man arofe,
And all its votaries commenc'd his foes.
Say, Prince Infernal, how inhanc'd thy ire,
When Jesus did his Whitfield's foul infpire;
When like a flaming Seraph round he flew,
Thy works, thy caufe, thy kingdom o'er-
    threw ?
                  Say,

Say ye celeftial Angels, how ye fled,

On willing wings, to guard his favour'd
      head:

Say, ev'ry Saint, how did your hearts rejoice,

When ere ye heard the found of W's voice ;

Well might each bofom figh, each Chriftian
      weep,

When this feraphic herald fell afleep.

But could we quit thefe tenements of clay,

And foar aloft into celeftial day,

There faithful Whitfield may at once be
      found,

With an eternal wreath of glory crown'd,

And fhouting loud Hofannahs to that God,

Who made him more than conqu'ror thro'
      his blood.

May we, like him, each breath for JESUS
      fpend,

Like Whitfield perfevere unto the end,
                    Like

Like him fail through this life's tempeftuous
    fea,
Fight the good fight, and gain the victory.
That when the laft tremenduous trump fhall
    found,
We in the wedding garment may be found,
With Angels, Saints, and favour'd Whitfield
    meet,
And ever worfhip at IMMANUEL's feet,
There fing the wonders of redeeming love,
With all the blood-bought company above.

On the Death of the Rev. Mr. HOWELL
    HARRIS, who died JULY 21, ~~1780~~ *1771*

WHAT penfive, folemn, dolefull tidings
    found?
All ZION's fons will deeply feel the wound!

A,

A brother, friend, a father dear is gone!
HARRIS is dead; his crown of glory's won!
What tongue can tell, what hand can paint
        the lofs
Of one fo fteady under JESU's crofs?

   Hail, happy foul! thy mourning days
        are o'er,
Inhabitant of mortal flefh no more!
No more fhall pain and anguifh thee confine,
Nor on a dying-bed thy head recline.
No more fhall fin opprefs thy righteous foul,
Nor grief come near, while endlefs ages roll.
No more (when glows thy heart with pure
        defire)
Thou'lt feel the force of perfecution's fire.
No more, with what is worfe, fhalt thou be
        try'd,
By vain Profeffors fetting thee afide :
                    Advanc'd

Advanc'd beyond their frowns, beyond their
　　-praife,
Harris with Angels tunes his grateful lays.
He fits with all thofe radiant hofts above,
And fwims in feas of pure celeftial love.
He meets his bleffed partner, gone before,
They meet to praife their God, and part no
　　more.
She like a brilliant diamond appears,
And helps to decorate the crown he wears.
Not her alone, but thoufands more there be,
Whom God awaken'd by his miniftry.
　　How glorioufly he fhines;—what mean
　　thefe fighs ?
Why flow thefe torrents from our languid
　　eyes ?
But ah ! we weep, that he from us fhould
　　part,
Who fo minutely trac'd the finner's heart ;

I　　　　　　Who

Who all the reafonings therein difclos'd,

And all the Devil's ftratagem's expos'd;

The man whom GOD firft raifed (in his
　　　youth)

In WALES, to propagate the Gofpel truth,

He fet his brow as brafs, no flefh he fear'd,

Effential truth he faithfully declar'd.

His grace, and knowledge, numbers to him
　　　drew,

They to his houfe, like doves to windows, flew,

Thoufands he caus'd, by the great pow'r of
　　　GOD,

To part with fin, and fly to JESU's blood,

He fpake, nor did his works his words deny,

He liv'd each day, as tho' that day to die.

　O Moon, and Stars, who make the dark-
　　　nefs light,

Tell us how oft he groan'd to GOD by night.

Say, rifing Sun, yea tell us dawning day,

How foon he left his bed, to praife and pray.

　　　　　　　　　　　　　　Say

Say walls, and clofets, ev'ry fecret place,
How oft he fupplicated GOD for grace,
How oft he with his bleffed Lord did meet,
And fill'd with love, bow'd at his facred feet.
Say, thou infernal Prince, how thou didft
  rage,
When HARRIS did againft thy caufe engage;
And let thine emiffaries here proclaim,
That mov'd by thee, they vilify'd his name.
Say ye bleft Angels, how difpatch'd from
  GOD,
To guard him round on ev'ry fide ye ftood,
Say, Sinners fay, how oft with warm defire,
He warn'd you to efcape eternal fire.
 Let towns and ftreets, houfes and fields
  proclaim,
His conftant ardour for his JESU's name.
Then let each Chriftian with a fecret figh,
Reverberate TREVECKA's penfive cry.

   Let

Let ev'ry heart lift up a fervent pray'r,
That old ELIJAH's mantle may be there.
That God from age, to age, may carry on,
Th' amazing work which HARRIS hath be-
  gun.
That all who fhall that Saint of God fucceed,
Like him, may prove true Ifraelites indeed.
 Not all the pow'rs of hell could him dif-
  may,
He to the end purfu'd the narrow way.
The paths of peace inceffantly he trod,
Then dy'd exulting in his Saviour God.
His fpirit catholic was friend to all,
Who Jefu's image bore, and name did call,
A mighty conq'ror as in life in death,
Cry'd vict'ry, vict'ry, to his lateft breath,
And tho' his body felt moft poignant fmart,
He faid " the dear Redeemer keeps my
  heart,"
         And

And when the great I AM fhall burn the
    fkies,
And bid unnumber'd Worlds to Judgment
    rife,
Then HARRIS by his Lord fhall be confeft,
And foul, and body, enter into reft,
Return triumphant to his deftin'd Throne,
And dwell with God, in extacies unknown.

On the Death of the Rev. Mr. WATKINS,
    of LANURSK, in the County of BRECON,
    who died the 9th of Jan. 1774.

Let me die the Death of the Righteous, and let my latter
End be like his.

ALAS! what mournful tidings ftrike my
    foul!
Ye Heav'nly Pow'rs, my paffions now con-
    troul,

WAT-

WATKINS is gone—is number'd with the
      dead!
And all his loving partner's joys are fled!
Now all his words affectionate and kind,
And ev'ry look is recent on her mind,
She views the token * of their mutual love,
And weeps there is no Father to reprove,
Who wifely rul'd with a paternal care,
And in her joys and griefs a part did bear.
Thus waves of grief acrofs her bofom roll,
And fill with deep diftrefs her penfive foul!
  But fhe alone doth not fuftain the lofs,
For ev'ry lover of the Saviour's crofs,
With whom he did in Chriftian union meet,
The death of WATKINS greatly muft regret.
In him they loft a brother and a friend,
On whom for counfel fage they might de-
      pend:

  * A Child about fix years old.

A kind reprover, but with all sincere,
Kind to the sinner, to the sin severe.
To speak essential truths he did not shun,
Not partial to the great,————
A faithful Monitor and Father he,
For gifts unequall'd in society;
A public Lab'rer, zealous for his God,
Who pointed sinners to the Saviour's Blood.
A blessed instrument thro' God hath been,
Of calling numbers from the paths of sin.
Belov'd of God, he did in God confide,
For " By his works his Faith was justi-
    fy'd."
Each truly Christian grace in him was found;
Oh! cruel Death, why didst thou give the
    wound,
Why didst thou not permit his useful days;
Who only liv'd to sound his Maker's praise?
                                    But

But ah! 'tis nature fpeaks, let Faith arife
And view the Saint afcending to the fkies;
His Lord for glory made his fervant meet,
Then call'd him hence to worfhip at his feet,
Hark! how the Heav'nly Choir began to
    fing,
A fong of praife, when WATKINS enter'd in.
To fee another of the blood-bought race,
Return'd from forrow, glory to embrace.
But oh! what extacies his foul poffefs'd,
When he beheld the glories of the blefs'd!
When he beheld, without a veil between,
What once as through a glafs was darkly
    feen!
His glorious Lord, in all his God-like
    charms!
And heard him, bid him welcome to his
    arms.

                " Come

" Come my belov'd by purchafe thou art
  mine,
" Be Life, eternal Life for ever thine."
  Thus fares the Saint, who while he dwelt
   below,
A world of fin and pain and grief did know,
Now he beholds among the ranfom'd few,
Thofe whom he lately in the body knew,
Who juft before him gain'd the happy fhore,
With joy they meet their Jefus to adore.
No noneffentials there the Saints difpute,
Nor will they wifh each other to confute,
Their only ftrife, who loudeft fhall proclaim
The matchlefs glory of the flaughter'd Lamb
Who has redeem'd us by his precious Blood
And made us Kings, and Priefts, and fons of
   God*.
  Children of God, who now the body wear,
Are not your hearts now panting to be there?

   * Rev. i. 5, 6.   Are

Are not your very inmoft fouls on fire,

Thus to be chanting with the heav'nly choir?

Your fpirit thus releas'd and foar away,

To dwell with WATKINS in eternal day.

Who would not like our lov'd EUSEBIUS die

Who when he found his diffolution nigh,

More than a conq'ror thro' his Saviour's
    Blood;

Could fay, " my life is hid with CHRIST in
    GOD!"

Commending all to JESU'S fpecial grace,

He fweetly bow'd his dying head in peace.

    Oh! why fhould we the death of Saints
      deplore

And mourn as tho' they dy'd to live no
      more?

Henceforth forbear to weep, but ftrive to
      raife

Our feeble pow'rs in GOD our Saviour's
      praife.   But

But tho' each Chriftian's heart might well
    rejoice,

When thus by death they hear their fove-
    reign's voice,

Let carelefs finners, aliens from their GOD,

Who never knew the worth of JESU's Blood,

With horror tremble, when in tender love

They hear the Saviour call his Saints above :

For when the laft * elect is gather'd in

Adieu ! to all the advocates for fin,   -

Adieu ! to ev'ry pleafure, fport, and game,

Except they find them in the gen'ral flame,

Then thofe who oft the good have vilify'd,

Shall be by GOD eternally deny'd.

When WATKINS in the number of the juft,

Shall find admittance, with a " Come ye
    bleft,"

" Enter the Kingdom, I prepar'd for you,

" Ere earth or fea their firft exiftence knew.

      * Matth. xx. iv. 31.

                   On

On the Death of the Author's Mother, Mrs. CAVE, of BRECON, who died Feb. 6, 1777.

And I heard a voice from Heaven, saying unto me, Write, Blessed are the Dead which die in the Lord, from henceforth: Yea, saith the Spirit, that they may rest from their Labours; and their works do follow them. Rev. xiv. 13.

'TIS done,—'tis GOD has call'd her—I submit,

And humbly own that best which he thinks fit.

But ah! when first I heard the direful news,

My wounded soul all comfort did refuse,

I heard—I felt—I sunk beneath the stroke,

With very grief my vital spirits broke.

I view'd the dear lov'd face, consign'd to death,

And

And heard her blefs me with her parting
    breath.
My heart was full, and in my grief I cry'd,
Oh! that I had with my dear Mother dy'd;
A thoufand of her foft endearing words
Flew to my mind, and pierc'd my heart like
    fwords.
She gave me birth, and more than twenty
    years,
I've been the object of her anxious cares.
Through helplefs infancy fhe fav'd from
    harms,
And nurs'd, and bore me in her tender arms.
She fympathiz'd in all my pain and grief,
And would have borne it all for my relief.

    And is that precious life for ever o'er ?
And fhall I know maternal love no more ?
In vain this vaft terreftrial ball I trace,
I view no more that lovely, deareft face :
No more her tender, Chriftian letters fee,
Nor hear how oft fhe wept, and pray'd for me.

       K   O

O worſt of days, that has bereft of life,
So dear a Mother, and ſo lov'd a Wife.
Where ſhall I go to eaſe my burthen'd heart?
Where find a friend, who'll with me bear a
      part?
Alas! there's none—O let me weep and ſigh!
I'll mourn, and wail my loſs until I die!

  Thus Nature felt, and ſpoke; for Reaſon
     fled,
And Faith, and Hope, lay bury'd with the
     dead;
But there's a GOD, a never-failing friend,
Whoſe pity, love, and goodneſs know no end:
I knew him ſuch, I to his footſtool flew,
And found his promiſes were firm and true.
He heard my ſad complaint, he gave relief,
And bade me riſe ſuperior to my grief.
Huſh—Nature—then I cry'd, nor more
     complain,
She only left a world of grief and pain,
                   To

To enter manfions of eternal reft,

To live, and reign with GOD for ever bleft.

How patient in affliction, how refign'd,

How meet for glory was her peaceful mind!

She welcom'd Death, and faid, *L O R D,*

   quickly come,

And take me hence, I long to be at home.

She bleft her houfe, and bid them ceafe to

  weep,

Then, with a fmile, in CHRIST, fhe fell

  afleep.

 Hail then, dear Saint, in thy immortal joy!

In blifs fuperlative, without alloy.

Live with thy GOD, nor let my partial mind

E'er wifh thy ftay from joys fo unconfin'd;

But let my grateful heart in praife afcend

To that all-gracious, all-victorious friend,

Who guided, lov'd, and kept thee to the

  end.

    K 2   EPITAPHS.

E P I T A P H S.

On a YOUNG MAN, who died Three Days
after he was married.

ALL flesh is grafs—Important truth !
Nor dare we boaft of health or youth,
The nuptial bed I fcarce had trod,
Ere fummon'd forth to meet my GOD,
Compell'd to leave my weeping Bride,
Sunk from her tender arms, and dy'd.

Another

Another, On a Young Lady.

BEHOLD ye thoughtlefs young and gay,
  What I am now, ye fhortly may.
I preach whilſt here I mould'ring lie,
And this my text—*Prepare to die !*

Another; On an Amiable Wife.

SHE's gone !—The dear companion of
      my bed,
And with her ev'ry earthly blifs is fled ;
An empty world is all I now can boaſt,
With her my ev'ry wiſh and joy was loſt.

P O E M S

ON RELIGIOUS SUBJECTS.

On hearing the Rev. Mr. R———d read
the Morning Service, and preach in
St. Thomas's Church, Winchester.

WHEN plac'd within the confecrated
        Ifle,

In penfive folitude I fat awhile;

At length with all the grace that Heav'n in-
        fpires,

All that folemnity the Church requires,

Began

Began the facred order of the day :
The Reverend R———d did each truth
    convey,
With fuch an emphafis as muft impart
A facred pleafure to each pious heart,
With fuch a cadence he difmifs'd each claufe,
As fhou'd enforce a GOD's eternal laws.

  Not as fome Priefts, who run o'er ev'ry
    pray'r,
As tho' no truth, or foul, or GOD were there.
The giddy hearer enters gay and vain,
And unaffected leaves the Church again ;
While leffer truths deliver'd on the ftage,
Or even fictions, will each mind engage,
Becaufe the player labours through his part,
To claim attention, and affect the heart.

  If in a tragic character he moves,
And treats of deaths, or difappointed loves,
       Then

Then all the horrors confequent on death,
Dart from his eyes, and fpeak in ev'ry breath.
Does he th' afflicted lover perfonate,
Then all that fofter paffion can create,
Solicitude—love—anguifh—grief—defpair,
Yea ev'ry figh, and languid look is there,
'Till each fpectator's eyes with tears o'erflow,
And thus concludes this fcene of fancy'd woe.

But truth's eternal, facred, and divine,
Where goodnefs, majefty, and juftice fhine;
Yea truths on which our future hopes de-
        pend,
Truths which the moft exalted mind tran-
        fcend;
That awful tragedy in which a God
Pray'd, agoniz'd, and bath'd the ground
        with blood;
That tragedy from which the Sun withdrew,
Nor wou'd his crucifying Maker view;
                That

That love,—ftupendous love,—furpaffing
    thought,
Which paid our ranfom, tho' fo dearly
    bought.
Thefe truths fublime the audience coldly
    hear,
Nor ever deign to drop a feeling tear;
While at the play each bofom heaves a figh,
Lo! in the Church unmov'd they fit,—But
    why?
The Prieft to whom the Embaffy is giv'n,
Who is the high Ambaffador of Heav'n,
Treats facred truth with cold indifference,
As tho' 'twere fiction, or impertinence.
Celeftial themes, that move a Seraph's lyre,
Droop on his tongue, and on his lips expire;
While the wife Actor aims by his addrefs,
Each fiction as undoubted truth t'imprefs.

                Would

Would thofe Divines, whom love canno
  induce,
Whofe languid hearts no ardor can diffufe,
(Whofe feet, perhaps, the church wou'd
  ne'er frequent,
If not infpir'd by her emolument),
Would even gain inftruction from the ftage,
By any means their audience to engage.
Left months and years fhould run their am-
  ple round,
And when the Mafter comes, no fruit be
  found.
No prodigal brought home, no fin fubdu'd,
No Saint advanc'd in grace, nor mind re-
  new'd.
All's barren ground, when an incenfed God,
Will from the Prieft require his people's
  blood.

         An

An Hymn in Time of Opposition.

O LORD a poor defpifed few,
    Once more together meet ;
Diftill on each thy heav'nly dew,
    And lay us at thy feet.

May each as the elect of God,
    Bowels of mercy know ;
And as the purchafe of thy blood,
    In all thy foot-fteps go.

Give us thy fpirit, gentle, mild,
    To teach us, Lord, that when
We are like thee, by man revil'd,
    Not to revile again.

And if we fuffer for thy caufe,
    O let us not repine,

                                   But

But simply *take*, and bear thy Crofs,
 And prove that we are thine.

Let no oppofing fpirit reign,
 But let us, through thy grace,
From all religious wars refrain,
 And follow after peace.

Thus let us by our works of love,
 Conftrain our foes to fay,
" We only feek our home above,
 And tread the narrow way."

Another Hymn.

COME thou all prevailing Spirit,
 Come and teach me how to pray,
Intercede for Jesu's merit,
 Wafh and take my fins away.

       How

How much need of that atonement,
   Hath a guilty foul like me?
Who am not one fleeting moment,
   From fome finful paffion free.

Sin, where e'er I go, I find it,
   Find it woven in my heart;
To thy crofs, O Jefus! bind it,
   Sin deftroy, and grace impart:
Sin, like weeds, for ever fpringing,
   Doth the foil throughout defile;
All my life's a life of finning,
   Oh! I'm viler than the vile.

Yes, I fin in ev'ry action,
   Sin in ev'ry word and thought;
I can't pray without diftraction,
   Sin, on all I do is wrote.
When I to my clofet enter,
   Seeking peace, in Jesu's blood,

L   Swift,

Swift, as thought, intrudes the Tempter,
 Drives, or draws, my heart from God.

Thus while I am proftrate lying,
 While my lips, in pray'r move,
While, with feeming ardour crying,
 For redemption, from above;
Lo! I find, at that dread inftant,
 My vain heart is rov'd away,
Wander'd off, on fomething diftant,
 And my lips alone do pray.

Then abafh'd, I filent wonder,
 Why is fuch a rebel fpar'd ?
Why not caft amongft that number,
 In eternal chains referv'd ?
Then with fhame and joy confounded,
 I exult in fovereign grace,
Grace which hath to me abounded,
 Me, the worft of Adam's race.

Lord,

Lord, if I forget to praiſe thee,
   Let my tongue forget to move;
Jeſu, to thy likeneſs raiſe me,
   Let me all thy goodneſs prove;
Let my guilt be now abſolved,
   My whole nature ſanctify,
Lord, I long to be diſſolved,
   Make me meet, and let me die.

On the Firſt General Faſt after the Commencement of the late War.

WHEN direful judgments pour in like
     flood,
And fields, alas! are drench'd with human
     blood,
When armies after armies proſtrate lie,
And brother, by his brother's hand muſt die,

When

When kingdoms feem to rife, or empire
    fall,
One great Omnipotent conducts it all,
And thofe have but a fuperficial fcan,
Who view no higher origin than Man.

  Be ftill, methinks I hear JEHOVAH cry,
Be ftill before your GOD, and know 'tis I!
'Tis I make peace, and I create ftern war,
And ride to battle in my flaming car,
I guide the bullet, point the glitt'ring fword
Defeat, or conqueft, wait my awful word.
But do I pleafure in deftruction take,
Or have your fins not bid the fword awake?
Do not a nation's fad offences call!
For national calamities to fall?

  Great Sov'reign Lord, we own thy judg-
    ments juft,
And hide our guilty faces in the duft;
                       Rejoice

Rejoice to hear a day is fanctify'd
T' implore thy aid, and humble BRITAIN's
    pride.
But may we not in this incur the rod,
And make a folemn mockery of GOD?
T'abftain from food, to take our prayer-
    books,
And walk to church with evangelic looks;
To bend the knee, or move the lips in
    pray'r,
If all the heart be not engaged there,
Is empty fhew, a poor external part,
While GOD, the Omnifcient GOD, demands
    the heart;
And fhould we fail in this grand facrifice,
The whole will be offenfive in his eyes.

    Defcend, celeftial dove, with holy fire,
And pure devotion ev'ry foul infpire.

May vital pray'r, exprefs'd by ardent fighs,
Afcend to God, and penetrate the fkies.
Let all the nation thus with fafting turn,
And heart fincere, their paft tranfgreffions
    mourn;
Then is eternal truth engag'd to blefs,
And crown our juft petitions with fuccefs.

The Author being requefted on a Sunday
    Evening, by a Company of gay Ladies, to
    write a few Lines of POETRY inftantane-
    oufly, fhe accordingly prefented them
    with the following.

WHEN you, good Ladies, bid me write,
    My drowfy Mufe had took her flight,
But ere fhe reach'd her moffy bed,
I gave a call, and back fhe fled.
                I humbly

I humbly afk'd her what to fay,
She anfwer'd—" On a fabbath day,
" If you prefume to write a line,
" Be careful that it is divine,
" For know that ev'ry word and thought
" Shall be to ftricteft judgment brought,
" And what is now tranfacted here,
" Shall to unnumber'd worlds appear;
" When Earth fhall from her center fly,
" And ftars defert the blazing fky,
" When frighted fouls in vain fhall call
" For rocks and hills on them to fall.
" Then let this day and night be fpent,
" As in that day you'll not repent."

A Poem,

A Poem, occafioned by hearing prophane
Curfing and Swearing.

AND can we wonder, if the fword
   Is plung'd in Brothers blood?
If threat'ning vengeance flies around
   From a tremendous GOD.

When daring finners thus prefume
   His anger to provoke,
When daily with impunity
   His dread command is broke.

What hath eternal truth declar'd,
   None guiltlefs fhall remain,
Who fwears by ought in Heav'n or Earth,
   Or takes his name in vain.

Yet imprecations fill our ftreets,
   And bold blafphemers dare

                       Invoke

Invoke damnation from above,
　And by JEHOVAH fwear.

Their impious breath pollutes the air,
　Omnipotence defies,
Compels a long forbearing GOD,
　In judgment to rife.

What! trifle with that facred name,
　Whofe goodnefs gives us breath!
Or Juftice fmites our feeble frame,
　And chains us down in Death.

Will not incenfed Majefty
　In vengeance lift his hand,
And bid deferved judgments fall
　On fuch a guilty land.

O when will finners ceafe from fin,
　And call for bleffings down?
Then fhall the fword be fheath'd again,
　And laurels deck the crown.

　　　　　　　　　　　On

On the Departure of Six Miffionaries to
AMERICA, foon after the Death of the
Rev. Mr. W.

WHEN once the foul, arifing from the
        dead,
Drinks the new wine, and eats the living
        bread,
It thirfts, it pants, it prays, for all to tafte
This heav'nly banquet, this celeftial feaft.
The bleft ambition this, the pray'r of thefe,
Who brave the dangers of the boift'rous
        feas.

    Go heralds, go! and may the God of
        peace
Go with you—guide you—ftrengthen you
        with grace.

                                Lo!

Lo! we commend you to his ſpecial care!

Go forth in confidence, your Lord is near.

Nor rocks, nor ſeas, nor raging billows
     dread,

His potent ſhield ſhall ſcreen each favour'd
     head.

Think how the winds and ſeas his voice
     obey'd

Your ſov'reign Lord! be not by ought diſ-
     may'd;

And whilſt on board, may JESUS be your
     guide,

In calmeſt ſeas, and o'er the rougheſt tide.

So ſhall each ſoul 'croſs the broad deep ſur-
     vive,

Till at the port deſir'd ye all arrive.

There, like young champions from great
     W—— ſprung,

Fly round, and gain for CHRIST a num'rous
     throng!

                       W——

W——— called thoufands, Jesus to adore!,
But may you call ten thoufand thoufands
  more!
Go forth like DAVID, with your fling and
  ftone,
And bear the world, and fin, and SATAN
  down,
Fight on courageous for your Saviour GOD,
Nor e'er recoil—atteft the truth to blood.
Stand firm, nor fear tho' men, or Devils
  frown,
Endure the Crofs, and wear the Heav'nly
  Crown.
O bleft Americans, how well might ye
Exult with utmoft joy, whilft penfive we
Sit forrowing here, and each to each deplore
Our abfent friends perhaps to meet no more.
O bleffed GOD! do thou our grief fuftain,
And let us know we have not heard in vain.
        Their

Their faithful exhortations bring to mind,
And teach us to revere thefe left behind.
And when this tranfitory life is paft,
O may we meet around thy throne at laft.
There, fill'd with love, our gracious God
   adore,
And weep, and figh, and part with friends
   no more!

On hearing the TOLLING of a BELL, in a
 very unhealthy Spring, when great Num-
 bers were carried off.

WHAT do I hear—or fancy that I
   hear?
(As long accuftom'd to the doleful found)
The tolling of yon melancholy bell!
Which has for weeks and months inceffantly

Some dreadful ftory in my ears proclaim'd,

And with repeated ftrokes alarm'd the town !

   Alas ! 'tis more than fancy——Hark it

       ftrikes !

Yea, more in language moft emphatical

It fpeaks—My inmoft foul with horror fills.

What does the dread but true informer fay?

What doth it intimate or what declare ?

Not that fome valiant chief, mighty in

       arms,

Returns, with honour and with conqueft

       crown'd :

Nor that a noble heir is lately born,

Whofe birth makes joyful his glad parents

       hearts,

And proves perhaps a blifs to future days :

Nor that the nuptial knot has juft been ty'd

Between fome happy pair, who mutually

Agree, to fpend their future days in love's

         Em-

Embrace—Nor is it what wou'd be lefs
    pleafing,
That fome intolerable woe is near, .
If an expedient be not quickly found
T'avert, or diffipate th'impending ftroke;
For were it thus, each may allay his grief,
And with a peradventure quell the figh..
But ah! it leaves us not one glimpfe of hope,
More than portention in its voice is heard.
It tells us that the fatal dart-is fled,
Lodg'd in the vitals, in the heart, or
    head,
Of fome one of the race of fallen Adam ;
And that an aweful feparation's made,
The fpirit forc'd from her clay tenement,
Prepar'd, or unprepar'd, away fhe's fled,
To ftand before the heart, rein-trying GOD.
And now her die eternally is caft
In fad perdition, or in endlefs blifs.

In vain ten thoufand arts would now com-
        bine,

Ten thoufand briny fhow'rs be pour'd in
        vain,

Or all the treafures of the Indies brought,

To make the foul refume her wonted feat,

Or actuate th' inanimated clay.

Such is the conqueft, fuch the pow'r of
        death,

Who daily fome new trophy doth erect,

To fhew how univerfally he reigns.

O thou inimitable King of Terrors !

Shall none efcape from thy voracious jaws,

But wilt thou ftill continue to deftroy,

Nor heed what age, what quality, or fex ?

The tender babe, the great, the wife, the
        good,

The hoary head, the mean, the weak, the
       .vile,

                    Are

Are all by thee, alike, reduc'd to duft !
Deftruction is effential to thy nature,
And formidable is thy very name.

But oh ! my foul why rageft thou at death ?
He is but the vicegerent of his GOD.
Nor did he ever give the mortal wound,
Until the fatal mandate had been feal'd,
And fent from the tremendous court of
   Heav'n :
And then, indeed, obfequious to his GOD,
And deaf to all the cries of finful man,
At once he executes the dread command.
'Tis Heav'ns decree, fince thy firft parents
   finn'd,
(And doft thou at the juft decree repine ?)
That ev'ry foul of man fhould pafs thro'
   death.
So, if thou traceft matters to their fource,
That monfter Sin was the efficient caufe

Of all calamities, of ev'ry death;
Of that for which I now hear yonder knell,
Which brings this fecret horror o'er my
   heart. •
Sinner awake, the deathly fignal hear,
Regard it as a monitor to thee!
A gracious call, a fpecial voice from Heav'n!
But ah! Death's vifits now fo frequent are;
Men laugh at Death, and lightly of him
  deem!
Tho' dead in fin, and enemies to GoD,
They think to meet him with an air of
  triumph;
Nor ever dream, that, at his dread approach,
Ten thoufand horrors will at once awake!
Confcience, tho' ftifled till that very moment,
Will like fome potent prince victorious rife,
And act the part for which it was defign'd.
Open the book of records, and arrange

      In

In dread array* before the sinner's mind,
Ten thousand times ten thousand past trans-
    gressions !
Which had for years as in oblivion laid,
(Then blacken'd with the thought of slighted
    grace,)
Will all appear—distract the guilty mind,
And drive the frantic soul to deep despair.
   Then with a fearful looking for of death,
She dies—and sinks into the dark abyss,
Nor ever knows a period to her pains.
For still, and still, and still, 'tis " wrath to
    come !"
O then vain man, " work while 'tis call'd
    to-day,"
Bethink thyself, before it be too late,
Fall quickly to soliloquy, and say——
Am I not mortal, like my fellow-creatures ?

* A law term, as well as military.

And

And can I call one inch of time my own,
Or boaft myfelf in the approaching hour ?
With great celerity my moments fly,
Surely my days will fhortly find a period !

Suppofe it now !—Bring Death's pale af-
pect near,
See him and his concomitants advance !
Fancy the well aim'd arrow on the wing,—
Sev'ring thy foul from all terreftrial things !
To ftand before the great tremendous Judge,
Whofe piercing eye hath taken cognizance
Of ev'ry thought, and word, and act, unjuft,
By thee committed, but by thee forgot !
Lo ! the minuteft has not mifs'd his notice,
Nor flipt the mind of the eternal all.

How ftands thy foul affected at the
thought ?
Ah ! is there not a fomething that recoils

And

And wifhes to poftpone the fatal hour ?

This argues all is not aright within :

And that if death fhould find thee as thou
    art.

Thou wouldft not die, as doth a bird, or
    beaft,

Who are annihilated at their death,

But dying, die, and die, and never die.

O then redeem thy time, to JESUS fly,

With fpeed take fhelter in his bleeding
    wounds,

Who only takes away Death's poignant fting

And turns the ghaftly monfter to a friend.

Make fure thy int'reft in the bleeding lamb,

Nor let him reft, until he fpeaks thee peace,

Then come whatever may, come life or
    death,

To live will then be CHRIST, to die be gain.

Death will be more defir'd by thy foul,

                Than

Than all the honours that the world bestows:
For by his friendly hand thou'lt part with sin,
And from a world of sorrow, grief, and pain,
To the immediate presence of thy GOD.
There bask in seas of uncreated bliss !
In extacies to worms on earth unknown !
With Angels and Arch-angels, sweetly join,
To sing the praises of a Triune GOD.

An HYMN for CONSECRATION, sung
at the Opening of the Countess. of *Hun-*
tingdon's Chapels in *Brecon*, *Worcester*, &c.

COME JESUS ! come, and bless this place !
   'Tis open'd in thy name ;
Descend with show'rs of heav'nly grace,
   And consecrate the same.

Eternal

Eternal God, our pray'r attend,
    Diffuse thy love around :
As to the burning-bush, descend,
    And make it holy ground !

Bid each the man of sin put by !
    As Moses did of old
His shoes put off, when he drew nigh,
    Thy glory to behold.

Lord, let thy glory fill this place,
    Yea fill each sinner's heart :
Come thou incarnate Prince of Peace,
    And never more depart.

In vain we are assembl'd here,
    If Jesus does not come :
Appear, thou bleeding Lamb, appear,
    Let ev'ry heart make room !

Within

Within thefe walls let thoufands, Lord,
   Thro' grace be born of thee ;
And in this place thy name record
    'Till time no more fhall be.

Now, Saviour, now thy work begin,
   Thy potent arm difplay :
Let fome poor rebel dead in fin
   Be made alive to-day !

Call fome poor wand'rer by thy grace,
   Who knew thee not before :
So fhall we blefs thee for this place
   When time fhall be no more.

An HYMN for CHRISTMAS.

AWAKE each heart, rejoice and fing,
   Salute the morn that CHRIST our King,
           Affumes

Affumes our flefh and blood ;
Sinners, 'twas life for you and me, .
When CHRIST partook our mifery,
   All hail the Saviour GOD !

IMMANUEL is the Saviour's name,
Yes GOD with us, O glorious theme !
   . Shout, fhout the news abroad,
With fpeed the wond'rous tidings tell,
A GOD defcends with Man to dwell !
   All hail the babe, the GOD !

The great I AM, who all things made,
The world's ftupendous pillars laid ;
   . Earth trembles at his nod :
Him whom eternal ages crown'd,
Is as an helplefs infant found :
   All hail the Saviour GOD !

O wond'rous! O amazing love!
Which brought the Saviour from above;
　　'Twas he the vine prefs trod!
His church's fins on him were laid,
And he the mighty debt hath paid:
　　All hail the babe, the God!

Bid Satan, felf, and fin depart,
Bid Jesus welcome to your heart,
　　He bore your wond'rous load;
In him the father's reconcil'd,
Well pleas'd alone in Mary's child,
　　All hail the Saviour God!

In grateful fongs your voices raife,
From fea, to fea, refound his praife,
　　Give, give the Saviour laud;
All Heav'n aftonifh'd ftands, that he
Should deign the fon of man to be,
　　To make us fons of God.

On

On the GENERAL FAST,

February 8, 1782.

OMNIPOTENT eternal all,
   By whom ſtates riſe or empires fall,
Whoſe potent word creates a world,
Or bids it be to atoms hurl'd.

Lord of all Lords, and King of Kings,
Beginning, center, end of things;
Fountain of light, of life, and love,
Through worlds below, and worlds above.

Wond'rous I AM, myſterious word,
Who canſt, or draw, or ſheath the ſword.
We reptiles, who of duſt are made,
Preſume to ſupplicate thy aid.

To thee we dedicate this day,
To mourn for sin, to fast and pray !
Thy wond'rous works of old declare
The great effects of fervent pray'r.

Does Moses but in spirit groan,
Lo! it prevails before thy throne.
The boist'rous waves at once divide,
And form a wall on either side.

Again he lifteth up his hands,
Israel a conqu'ring army stands:
But when his fervent spirit fails,
They fall, and Amaleck prevails.

The Ninevites its influence knew,
And jointly to thy footstool flew:
They mourn, they fast, to Heav'n they cry,
And turn th' impending judgment by.

May

May we like them confeſs our ſin,
The renovating work begin,
Timely avert thy vengeful rod,
And Jacob-like prevail with GOD!

Our land, our ſinking land protect,
Our king and ſenators direct;
Our fleets preſerve, our armies bleſs,
And bid the nation ſhout ſucceſs.

Our foes, our envious foes annoy,
And all their impious plots deſtroy.
Let peace her wiſh'd for banner ſpread,
And laurels deck our ſov'reign's head.

On

On hearing the Rev. Mr. B——— from

PSALM 65, 2.

O thou that heareſt Prayer, unto thee ſhall all fleſh come.

WITH calm attention lo! I heard,
My heart the ſage divine rever'd;
While he with holy zeal explain'd
The gracious words his text contain'd.
I'll bid the muſe the theme prolong,
And fórm the ſubſtance in a ſong.

To GOD the Lord ſhall man repair
By public and by private pray'r;
Thus humbly his dependance own
On thee, thou infinite, unknown.
Where two or three are met in pray'r,
Lo! GOD has promis'd to be there;

He's

He's there a prefent help to blefs,
Crown each petition with fuccefs,
Or in his wifer way our wants redrefs.

 If warm'd by pure devotion's fire,
We to our clofet fhould retire,
There, unperceiv'd by human eye,
Pour forth to GOD our plaintive cry,
Or fend before the throne a contrite figh,
Lo! he'll on wings of love defcend,
And to our various wants attend.
Here we may get our hearts renew'd,
And each unruly luft fubdu'd:
Here virtue draw from JESU's blood,
And hold fweet intercourfe with GOD:
Here we may all our griefs reveal,
Nor one beloved fin conceal;
For, e'er we fpeak, Omnifcience knows
What all our words and tears difclofe;

       Then

Then fome celeftial cordial gives,
And lo! the contrite finner lives.

Not all the wealth the Indies own,
Crowns or the moft exalted throne,
Shou'd counterpoife the blifs of pray'r,
When God is by his prefence there.
In pray'r feraphic joys we find,
Which quite transform the earthly mind.
The man who always, ere he pray'd,
From the bright path of duty ftray'd,
Lo! now he gladly runs therein,
And hates the garments ftain'd by fin.

This change is in himfelf alone,
For changes are to God unknown,
(Fixt as his own eternal name)
To-day and yefterday's the fame:
With endlefs glory to reward
Each humble follower of the Lord;

And

And fixt his purpose to disdain
The soul who will in sin remain,
Who slights the offers of his grace,
And never bows to seek his face.

As soon may man by air exist,
Or brutes without their food subsist;
The feather'd warblers live in floods,
Or the finn'd tribes amid the woods;
As soon may Satan burn with love,
Or God a fount of envy prove,
As shall the soul to heav'n ascend,
Who without pray'r his days shall end.

When man has misimprov'd his time,
And spent his youth, and health, and
    prime,
Only his God to disobey,
When Death advances, he may pray,
But then his pray'r may be in vain,
God justly may his suit disdain;
                 He

He may, 'tis true, his grace extend,
And ev'n in death commence his friend:
So let the dying not defpair,
But oh! let all the living fear;
For on an awful chance depends
A world of blifs that never ends.
God may accept—and he may not—
He may thy name for ever blot
Out of his book of life divine,
And thy fad foul to Hell confign.

Then form your hearts in health to pray,
Nor let appearances difmay
Your feeking fouls :—Tho' good men lie
On beds of languifhment, and die,
And tho' the wicked feem to rife
On tow'ring pinions to the fkies,
Think not the juft has no reward,
Or is forgotten by his Lord,

Or

Or that his wrath does not remain
On thofe who do his grace difdain:
The wicked lives but to fulfil
The direful meafure of his ill;
Each day ftill makes the finner worfe,
And life by fin becomes a curfe;
The greater his iniquity,
The more his punifhment will be.
The good man dies, leaves earth and pain,
A crown of glory to obtain;
And if thro' life God try'd his grace,
'Twas but his glory to increafe.

Let man before his God be ftill,
Pray with fubmiffion to his will:
If what we afk be for our good,
'Twill not be by our Lord withftood;
But if he e'er our fuit denies,
'Twas wrong—for he's immenfely wife.

Nature

Nature wou'd aſk for health and reſt,
When pain and ſickneſs may be beſt,
Our droſſy nature to refine ;—
If ſo, be pain and ſickneſs mine.
The chaſt'ning rod I'll ne'er deſpiſe,
'Tis a rich bleſſing in diſguiſe.

Be thus reſign'd and paſſive found,
In works of holineſs abound.
Let ev'ry word, and work, and thought,
Be into ſtrict obedience brought ;
But here beware of a miſtake,
Leſt that be fatal which you make.
Think not by this thy Heav'n to gain,
Or all thy righteouſneſs is vain ;
Nought but a Saviour's precious blood
Can give thy ſoul acceſs to GOD ;
Nought but his ſpotleſs righteouſneſs,
(And not thy works) muſt be thy dreſs.

'Twas

'Twas he that firſt thy ſoul inſpir'd,
Thy heart with pure devotion fir'd;
He gave thee faith, and faith's increaſe,
Purchas'd thy pardon, ſeal'd thy peace,
And bid thee live and grow in grace.
He is the firſt, and he alone
The laſt, the great, and corner ſtone;
Who builds upon this rock ſhall ſtand,
Who builds without it, builds on ſand,
And be his fabrick ne'er ſo tall,
'Twill in the day of trial fall.

Then wou'd you live and learn to die,
Live holy, yet your works decry;
And only hope a ſeat above,
Thro' boundleſs grace and dying love.

INGRATITUDE.

INGRATITUDE—thou fin accurft,
  Of ev'ry fin pronounc'd the worft;
Detefted weed, where e'er thou'rt found
Infernal poifon fwells the ground.

Chriftians, who at perfection aim,
Or to its facred heights attain,
God-like in all they act or fay,
Injuries with kindneffes repay.

Heathens, who led by nature's rays,
Nor ever bleft with gofpel days,
By nature's dictates underftood,
'Twere juft to render good for good.

Brutes, that of reafon ne'er poffeft,
Can act no higher than a beaft,
Led by their own revengeful will,
Will doubtlefs render ill for ill.

But

But thou accurſt, where e'er thou art,
Conſcience will know and point the dart ;
Thou who repayeſt *good* with *evil,*
Art only equall'd by the Devil.

An **HYMN** for a **CHILD** who has loſt its
FATHER or MOTHER.

O Thou who once didſt children bleſs,
   And take them in thy arms,
Defend the infant fatherleſs,
And guard my feet from harms.

Thou canſt the loſs of friends ſupply,
   And turn to good each ill ;
Tho' ev'ry friend ſhould fail or die,
   Thou art all gracious ſtill.

Thy

Thy wifdom and thy pow'r I own,
  For all thy ways are juft;
The prince thou raifeft to his throne,
  Or lay'ft him down in duft.

May I obey thy facred word
  In thefe my infant days;
Grow up in all things like my Lord,
  And learn to lifp his praife.

So fhall I find thy promis'd reft,
  When this frail life is o'er,
And meet in my dear Saviour's breaft
  My friends fled hence before.

LOVE,

L O V E,

The ESSENCE of RELIGION.

NOT every one who crieth Lord,
 Or hear, or pray, or preach thy word,
Wilt thou in God-like accents own,
Or hail as partners of thy throne.

What if this sect or that I join,
Believe my party most divine,
Vain will my warmest notions prove,
If abfent from my heart, thy love.

What if with Calvin I agree,
Or to Arminian doctrines flee,
I ftill remain a child of fin,
If love does not prefide within.

Let

Let bigots for the fhell contend,
In idle controverfies fpend
Their precious time, who zealots fire
And notions (not thy love) infpire,

With me let names and parties fall,
Thy love, my fov'reign God, my all;
The fubftance this:—Of this poffeft,
'Mid flaming worlds I ftand confeft.

F I N I S.

ERRATA.

Page 8, Line 2, *for* tears, *read* tares
    64, last Line, *for* Inæther, *read* In æther
    78, Line 6, *for* propogate, *read* propagate
    83, *for* 1781, *read* 1771.
    108, Line 1, *for* talk, *read* take
    109, Line 4, *for* simple, *read* sinful
    114, Line 2, *for* took, *read* tak'n
        Line 7, *for* bid, *read* bade
    120, Line 10, *for* the, *read* tho'
    124, Line 13, *for* vexatious, *read* voracious

ADVERTISEMENT.

WHEREAS the Printer of this Work did engage with the Author, that it should be printed and compleatly finished, in an elegant, masterly manner, on a new type and good paper, all the same sort, size, and colour. Therefore, if upon inspection it is found not answerable to the above engagement, the Printer has violated his agreement, deceived and disappointed the Author, and is wholly accountable for the defect.

www.ingramcontent.com/pod-product-compliance
Lightning Source LLC
Chambersburg PA
CBHW031109020726
47495CB00007B/2121